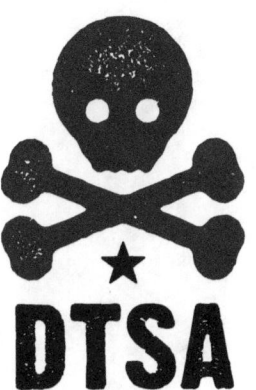

For artist resources and worksheets
to accompany this book, visit:
www.DeathToTheStarvingArtist.com

For more about the author and his art, visit:
www.NikolasAllen.com

DEATH TO THE STARVING ARTIST

Art Marketing Strategies for a Killer Creative Career

by Nikolas Allen

Cover Illustration by **Mimi Isbell**

Cover Layout & Design, Author Photo Illustration,
Book Layout and Title Page Graphics by **Nikolas Allen**

Expressions of Gratitude to:

Brenda Woods, my partner in crime and biggest supporter.

Arthur Cronos, for treading the book-publishing path before me and encouraging me to follow suit.

Jessie Zapffe, she worried about the title, she worried about the colors, but hey–that's just what mothers do. I love you Mamasan.

Editor savant, **Nate Dorward**, for improving the clarity of this book and teaching me a few things in the process.

This book is dedicated to the creative souls who pursue their passions in an effort to express their talent, share their gifts and shine their light on the world. Never stop believing in yourself.

Contents

"Why do people think artists are special? It's just another job."

—Andy Warhol

Introduction: The Path of an Artist

I've been involved in the arts all my life. As a kid, inspired by *MAD* magazine, I would spend hours drawing cartoon characters and comic strips. That changed at age 12, when I discovered KISS and started playing guitar. I was playing in bar bands by age 18, and pursued rock stardom in various bands for the next dozen years.

Luckily, I also decided to go to school for Advertising Design and started my career in advertising while simultaneously chasing my musical dreams. I was hired by The Musicland Group as an art director in 1997. They were coming out of financial difficulty and brought me on board to help them with their brand positioning. This job was a match made in heaven, since they were all about music and entertainment and so was I.

In 2000, I wrote a commercial that was produced for Sam Goody music stores, which was a brand extension of Musicland. After being involved in every aspect of the production, I fell in love with the motion-picture medium and decided to dive head-first into the field of video production.

I was still playing in bands at that time, but I knew that if I was going to pursue my new passion, then something else had to give. I figured, since I had spent half my life on the pursuit of musical success, I was ready to focus my attentions elsewhere.

I quit my band, quit my job at Musicland and started a video production company, Digital_Renegade. I also freelanced as a graphic designer for select clients in order to supplement my income during the lengthy film production cycles.

1

I submerged myself in the world of indie filmmaking, producing short films, music videos and commercials. My plan was to create a killer reel of work, be "discovered" and either get financed to create my own larger-budget projects or get hired for high-buck directing gigs in Hollywood. But after seven years of hard work on long projects with short budgets, I was burnt out. Hollywood had not come calling, so I folded the company and moved my focus to art and apparel.

I've always been obsessed with style and fashion, so I decided to create an edgy-but-cute line of screenprinted apparel for women, Renegade Girl Grafik Garments. I launched an online boutique to sell them, which taught me the basics of e-commerce and blogging. At the same time, I started producing my own collection of contemporary pop art.

Unfortunately, I launched my fashion line in 2008 just as the economy was starting to tank, and after two years of hard work trying to build a new clothing brand during a recession, I decided to cut my losses and pull the plug on the e-commerce site.

I turned my entire focus on the creating, marketing, exhibiting and selling of my unique brand of contemporary pop art. So far, I've exhibited and sold my artwork in Minnesota, Oregon and California, and I'm currently targeting more select hot spots up and down the West Coast.

I feel fortunate to have pursued the dreams, ideas, passions, careers and plans that have moved and inspired me over the years. Since I have acted on all my creative desires, I don't have any "wish-I-did" or "should've done" regrets haunting me.

Have I been successful? Definitely. Have I experienced failure? Indeed.

Some ventures proved more financially successful than others, but the intangible skills, enjoyment, collaboration and experience that I gained from each business venture and creative pursuit—even the ones that didn't work out as planned—has always proved to be well worth the time, energy, effort and resources I devoted to it.

While I was recouping from the failure of my clothing line, which happened to coincide with a move across the country, I started focusing on "what's next." This seems to be an oddly common trait among entrepreneurs: no matter how badly you crash and burn, you're always excited about the next adventure.

I had the epiphany that it would be a far more noble pursuit to share my knowledge and passion for branding, marketing and advertising with other artists and entrepreneurs who are struggling with the same issues that I have faced throughout my career, rather than focusing it entirely on my own endeavor. After all, I believe it is through serving others that we come closest to achieving our true purpose in life.

That epiphany begat the launch of my company, BAM! Small Biz Consulting, which led to my art-marketing workshops, which led to this book, which will hopefully lead to your greater success.

My intention is to educate, encourage and inspire ambitious creatives—whatever their artistic medium or discipline—with ideas, insights and resources that will motivate them to strategically market themselves and their art both online and off, which is paramount in maximizing the chances of success in any creative field.

One thing you will notice about this book is that it's made up of many short, easily-digestible paragraphs. This is not to pad the book so it has more pages; it's to make it easy for you (and me) to read. This format was inspired by the blogs I've been reading and writing for the past five years, which are formatted to be scannable, as opposed to having walls and walls of text like typical books do. I also understand that people have short attention spans, and since this book is packed with tons of useful, practical information, I wanted to deliver it in a way that would be easy to read and assimilate.

Are you ready? Let's do this!

PROLOGUE:
PLANNING YOUR JOURNEY

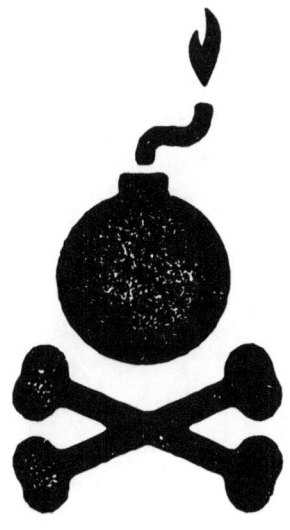

P.1

Essential Attributes for Success

Throughout my life and career, I have always worked with people who are pursuing their creative dreams: musicians, designers, copywriters, filmmakers, actors, photographers, models and artists all trying to make a living doing what they love to do.

Many have attained varying degrees of success. Others continue to work jobs they are not passionate about, while they pursue their creative dreams on the side. There is nothing wrong with doing it this way. Depending on your own financial obligations and responsibilities, it's imperative to generate income elsewhere if it's not yet coming from your art. However, it is also imperative to believe that it IS possible to transition your art from a part-time passion to a full-time career. We'll talk more about your options when we discuss career objectives.

There is a popular belief that making a living as an artist is not feasible, or that people can be good at EITHER art OR business, but not both. Often these ideas and beliefs come from outside sources, but sometimes these roadblocks exist even in the artist's own mind.

In order to break down these limiting beliefs, one needs to possess the following essential attributes:

Confidence in yourself and your work.

I can't stress enough the importance of confidence. You can only be a success if you believe it to be possible. The "inner critic" that resides in the head of every artist is strong and loud. Not to mention the real critics in the outside world who are more than happy to tell you what is "wrong" with your work.

These antagonistic forces must be offset by a healthy dose of confidence. This doesn't mean you need to adopt the "arrogant artist" cliché; rather, it means you are confident enough in your creative expression that outside criticism doesn't reduce you to a weeping sack of self-pity. Instead, you listen to this feedback, determine which to consider and which to ignore, and proceed accordingly.

Motivation to move toward your goals relentlessly.

You are the only one responsible for defining and pursuing your own version of success. Taking a passive approach to your art career (i.e., waiting for the art rep, rich patron or gallery to pluck you from obscurity) ain't gonna cut it. Whether you actively seek out existing opportunities or create them yourself, you must take a proactive approach to your career.

Know your goals and utilize them daily, weekly, monthly, yearly to fuel your continual drive towards your own version of success. Allow your goals to morph and change over time if need be, and redefine them as necessary, so they remain a relevant driving force throughout your life.

Discipline to keep striving and creating over the long haul.

When the going gets tough—and it will—the disciplined keep going. They push beyond their comfort zone, keep their eyes on the prize and keep moving forward, head down, arms swinging, day after day after day.

It's hard enough to be disciplined when it comes to creating your art. When you add the consistent effort necessary to market your work, contact galleries, schedule, install and promote exhibits, network and follow-up with prospects and contacts, it becomes clear that epic levels of discipline are required.

Quite frankly, it's very difficult. That's why there are so many "starving artists" out there. Success requires tons of effort and a little luck. Focus on what you can control—the effort—and let the forces beyond your control take care of the luck.

Desire to view your work as a "business."

Embracing this concept is a huge hurdle for many artists. Any type of creative activity is a sacred act of self-expression. When making art, you are connecting with your own higher intelligence. You are tapping into the universal creative spark in order to transmute "nothing" (the blank canvas of an idea) into "something" (a work of art).

Wow! That's some heavy stuff. How are you going to put a price tag on that?

Well, the truth is, you don't HAVE to. There are many artists who don't want to "dirty their hands" with money and business where their art is concerned. They loathe the thought of "selling out" and fear that adopting business and marketing tactics will only lead to "prostituting" themselves and their work. For these artists, the ACT of creating is their reward and that alone is the reason they do it.

I can respect that position. It is not my intention to try to change these people's minds. However, these are not the people I'm trying to reach with this book.

I want to reach people who are ready to apply—to themselves and their art—the same effective business principles being utilized by successful companies and entrepreneurs.

I want to reach people who are willing to work just as hard at marketing their art as they are at creating it. I want to reach people who don't think "marketing" is a dirty word and who realize that creating art, while certainly a sacred act of self-expression, can also be a rewarding route towards self-employment.

Accepting Feedback and Criticism

Think about your work as an artist. Do you know where your strengths are? How about your weaknesses? Are you able to take advice, criticism and feedback? As I mentioned earlier, it's very important to have confidence in yourself and your work. It's equally important to be able to handle outside opinions with grace.

I will admit that this is a struggle. Especially in the beginning of one's career, it's easy to think that you know what's best and already have all the right answers. Sometimes, our fear of appearing "stupid," "dumb," "naïve" or inexperienced will cause us to reject advice, outside help, suggestions and opinions.

It took me a long time in the advertising field to realize that, occasionally, outside opinions could actually improve my work. You mean MY solutions aren't always the best? Imagine that!

The Japanese Zen Buddhist Shunryo Suzuki-Roshi said, "In the beginner's mind there are many possibilities, but in the expert's there are few."

Maintaining a Beginner's Mind throughout your career, regardless of your level of experience, will allow you to be receptive to external ideas and open to unexplored possibilities.

People love to offer opinions and advice. When they do, thank them for it. While a good, passionate art debate is often invigorating, it can easily devolve into a heated argument with personal attacks and hurt feelings. Therefore it's important to remember that there's no need to take a defensive stance or to try proving anyone "right" or "wrong." After all, everyone is allowed their own opinions, no matter how ridiculous they may be.

Even though you have invested much more time, effort and thought into your creative work than the first-time viewer has, it is still important to consider the validity of their opinions and ideas before deciding whether you should implement or ignore them.

Planning Your Career Goals

Creating a plan for your course of action is essential. Since goals and plans often change, you should continue to revisit and revise your career goals throughout your life. Only when you define your own idea of success, can you measure your progress as you work toward your goals.

When setting goals, it's helpful to utilize the SMART acronym. SMART goals are Specific, Measurable, Attainable, Realistic and Timely.

Specific – Be as specific as possible when stating your goals. When you have a clear idea of what you want the end result to be, you have a better idea of the precise steps you need to take in order to get there.

For example: Let's say your goal is to be a freelance illustrator. That's a pretty general goal. It doesn't speak to your unique strengths, artistic style or niche market and it may be hard to decide where to focus your promotional efforts.

A more specific goal might be: I want to be a freelance illustrator specializing in celebrity portraiture for fashion and entertainment magazines. This will indicate what your portfolio should showcase and which magazines you'll need to target with your inquiries and promotional materials.

Measurable – By working units of measurement into your goals, you are able to manage your progress and keep yourself on track. If your goals are large, you can break them up into a series of smaller ones. As you achieve each small goal, you can see how close you are getting to the finish line, which is both satisfying and inspiring. Then, if you happen to get derailed at any point, you will know where you went astray and know where to refocus your efforts when you're ready to start up again.

Measurable goals contain numbers and state "how many" or "how often" you will be taking action.

For example: I want to stage three solo exhibits this year and be in four group shows. Or, I will submit work to eight magazines this month. Or, I will create ten paintings for my new series.

Attainable – Thinking big is great. I'm all for big ideas, big plans and big goals. However, if you set your sights too high right away, the process and the journey can seem arduous and overwhelming. The bigger the plans you make, the bigger the challenges you face, which may cause you to abandon your goals in frustration regardless of the progress you may have made.

It's better to take small steps and set goals that match your current level of skill, knowledge and ability. When you achieve each of your smaller goals, your skills sharpen, your experience accumulates and your confidence increases. As this happens, the goals you set naturally become progressively more challenging, yet continually attainable.

Realistic – This goes along with being attainable. There's often a hierarchy of steps necessary to reach some of your big goals. So, if you're holding out for that exhibit at MoMA, coverage in the *New York Times*, or the position of creative director at a top agency, you may be missing out on some valid opportunities in the present that will help prepare you for these larger goals in the future. The above goals may very well be attainable, but only when your level of skill and experience aligns with the requirements necessary to achieve them.

Accept that your career is a long journey. You don't need to race to the finish line; just start where you are and enjoy each milestone, each event and each opportunity along the way. Celebrate each success as it occurs while accepting and learning from your failures and disappointments. Keep moving forward with confidence, and be realistic about where you are in relation to the skills and experience necessary to achieve your larger goals.

Timely – Every goal that you set should be accompanied by a general timeline of when you want to achieve it. The timelines you set are going to depend on what else is going on in your life, how much time you have to devote to achieving the goal and what the goal actually is.

If you want to stage an art exhibit, first you need to make sure you have a full body of work prepared. It's very stressful to be up against a deadline when you're not quite ready for it. On the other hand, it can be quite motivating, but racing to finish creative work in order to open a show usually means the quality is going to suffer.

When applying timelines to your goals, be sure to give yourself just enough time to put in the right amount of research, work, effort and promotion necessary. While setting timelines too tight can be stressful, setting them too loose and lenient often doesn't provoke a sense of urgency that will motivate you to take action. This leads to procrastination, which means either the goal never gets accomplished or, in the case of an impending exhibit, you end up leaving everything to the last minute and creating shoddy work.

Only you know how much time you have to dedicate to the actions you need to take in order to meet your goal. Eventually, with experience, you will learn what your productive threshold is and how long things generally take to happen. Set your timelines accordingly.

Defining Your Career Objectives

If you don't know where you are going, any road will take you there. Defining your career objectives helps you determine which is the best route to take in order to reach them. Many opportunities will arise throughout the course of your life. Some will be perfect for the advancement of your creative career and others may be a detour that sidetracks your momentum, an alternate route that takes you off the most direct path, or even a dead-end that wastes your time and gets you nowhere.

When you have a clear destination, you are better able to gauge which opportunities to pursue and which to disregard. Obviously, you never really know what the future outcome of anything will be, but your clarity will increase your chances of choosing the opportunities that act as stepping stones towards your greater goals.

In order to get a clearer understanding of where it is you want to go, ask yourself the following questions when planning your goals and objectives:

What does your desired lifestyle look like? There are many artists who want their art to provide only a partial income. Perhaps they've got important family and job obligations or time restraints, or they simply don't want to go all-out in pursuit of an art career.

Other artists may be ready to dive head first into their creative career and maximize their output, earnings and success. So,

14

while it's imperative to know what you want out of your career, it's equally essential to know what you DON'T want.

Are you capacity-limited? How much can you feasibly produce? If you don't have a full body of work yet, you probably don't want to schedule a solo show. Also, as you start selling pieces, you want to make sure you have time to produce new works, especially if you already have bookings in the future.

As your momentum starts building, you want to be able to capitalize on that forward motion, instead of stalling right at the on ramp because the public demand outweighs the creative supply. The public may wait patiently for a "big name" artist to produce her next series, but up-and-comers need to be ready to strike while the buzz is hot, or the public will move right along.

Some artists are quite prolific, creating new works quickly and easily. Others have a long, thoughtful creation process that limits the amount of work they produce within a certain timeframe. As you move forward with your creative career, know which working style you possess so you can plan your 'create–exhibit–market–repeat' cycles accordingly.

How far are you willing to travel? With many artistic disciplines, such as music, dance, and theater, if you are not physically present on opening night, there is no show. In these cases, travel is part of the job and, if you expect to make any headway in the field, you arrange your life around your travel schedule.

In other cases, such as fine art or film, the work can go on tour without you. However, it's certainly a best practice to be present at your own openings. While not always possible, it allows an artist to maximize the opportunity to connect with an audience, get real-time feedback, build relationships, and increase the network of interested contacts.

In 2008, I was living in San Francisco, and I scheduled a solo show several months out. A month later, I ended up moving five hours north to the upper tip of California. So, when showtime came, I drove my art down to SF, stuck around for a few days to set up the show and attend the opening, then drove home. When the show ended, I had to do the same thing to pick up my work.

I did sell some work during the show's run, but I spent far more money and time just to make the show happen than I brought in from my sales. So, from a creative standpoint, the show was great, but from a business standpoint, it was a lousy endeavor that did not return on my investment. This is why it's imperative to know your objectives: if you're trying to break into a new area or market, the occasional dicey investment might be worthwhile, providing it evens out in the long term. However, if you make a habit of spending more on your shows than you bring in from your sales, you will never break out of the starving artist paradigm.

How far are you willing to ship? It's always exciting to stumble across a Call to Artists announcement that speaks directly to your style from a high-end gallery in a great art city. It's less exciting when you have to pack and ship your work across the country, which can be quite expensive and more than a little nerve-wracking.

Of course, it's a very common practice and, as your career takes off, it will make sense to target better galleries in better cities than those in your own vicinity. Plus, there are specialized art-shipping companies that will transport your work if you don't want to rely on the commercial shipping companies, which have a tendency to mistake your precious cargo for a basketball.

However, let me state for the record that I am not a fan of shipping my babies to faraway lands to be cared for by strangers. In the higher-end galleries, there are plenty of upstanding curators and gallery directors who will take excellent care of the work and use their best visionary talent to create an amazing exhibition. As for the alternative art spaces, second- and third-tier galleries, and non-profits, well let's just say that, personally, I prefer to physically BE there with my work, to see the space, to pitch in and help out when appropriate.

Plus, opening night best practice requires the artist to attend the reception. You are the only one responsible for greeting the public, discussing your work, networking and making sure people are signing your mailing list. If you do not attend the opening, you are missing out on a key opportunity to connect with your audience. Sure, someone from the gallery can speak for you in your absence, but keep in mind that YOU are your own best marketing vehicle.

What's your price structure? Pricing artwork seems to be one of the biggest hurdles artists face when they start exhibiting their work. When it comes to determining the price of your work, there is no one "right" way to do it. However, some of the factors that should be considered are: how long it takes you to create the work (i.e., what is the value of your time?), cost of the materials used, what other artists at your level are charging, how you want to position yourself (are you a Kia or a Cadillac?), and what price points are currently selling in the market.

I was the marketing director for Liberty Arts Gallery, a contemporary fine art gallery in northern California, for two and a half years. During my tenure, I installed dozens of art exhibits and saw a variety of pricing strategies. Some of the true beginners pluck a random number out of thin air, which is often so low that I wonder if it even covers their materials. Others are eternally hovering in the $200–500 range, which probably feels like a safe, sellable number. Then there are the more established artists who price their work up into the thousands.

Another strategy is to price the originals quite high, and sell prints of the work at an affordable price point. Some artists feel this a bastardization of their work, but in my mind, it's better to sell ten prints for $100 each than NOT sell the $1,000 original because it's out of a buyer's price range.

There are also instances when a particular piece is so special or sentimental to the artist that they don't want to sell it at all, yet they still want to share it through exhibition. In this case, they indicate that their piece is NFS, or Not For Sale. This is perfectly acceptable, but hopefully you have plenty of other work that IS selling, in order to make up for the pieces that aren't generating income.

Before you start submitting work for exhibition, do your research and be certain you have a comfortable pricing structure in place. It's not the gallery owner's responsibility to tell you what your art is worth; it's yours. So determine your prices and state them confidently whenever you are asked.

The Marketing Process

Once you have identified your career objectives, created a strong body of work, and considered all the points and questions above, it is time to start marketing your work. It's vital to realize that marketing is not something you trot out whenever you need to promote a show; rather, it is an ongoing process that needs to imbue your thoughts, words and actions as you embark on the journey of your creative career.

Just as your creative imagination is always hovering in your consciousness, waiting to come alive through a creative spark of inspiration, your strategic marketing mind should be equally accessible at any given time. This may seem difficult or even undesirable at first, but just as your artistic talent took time to nurture and develop, your business skills deserve the same attention. As those skills advance, it will become easier to find a comfortable balance between creative activity and strategic activity.

There's a well-known definition of marketing that describes it as "the process of getting people to know, like and trust you." Small business marketing guru John Jantsch, who runs Duct Tape Marketing, has added two more essential elements to the mix: "to buy from you, and refer you to others."

Therefore, as an artist who wants to market your work for a successful career, you need to get people to know and like you and your work, to trust your character and your quality, to buy your work, and to refer other people to your work.

Taking the above objectives into consideration, I have distilled the marketing process into three distinct components that need to align in order to be successful: using the Right Tools, to reach the Right Audience with the Right Message.

Each of these elements requires deeper exploration to maximize its full potential, but together, they are the key to achieving success with your marketing strategy. Let's examine how each applies to you and your career and attempt to put together a cohesive plan that will take you to the next level with your marketing.

Note: If you're already feeling a bit overwhelmed by all the questions, I have produced an accompanying workbook that will help keep you on track. Fill it out and use it as a blueprint to guide you on your way to success!

 **Download the free DTSA Workbook to create your own custom art-marketing strategy:**
www.DeathToTheStarvingArtist.com/workbook

PART I
THE RIGHT MESSAGE

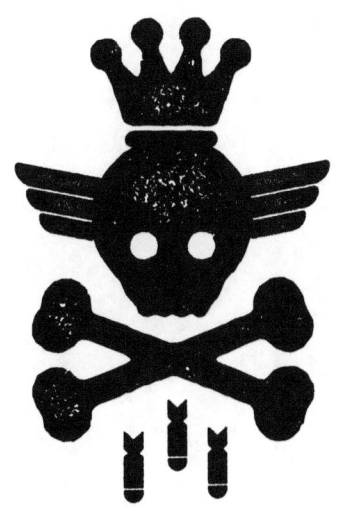

1.1

Creating the Right Message

When it comes to marketing, you'll hear a lot of talk about your "message" or your "messaging." When I'm speaking with clients, or writing blog posts and articles, I often talk about the significance of creating a Meaningful Marketing Message. After all, there is so much advertising noise out there competing for attention that you need to make your message truly meaningful if you hope to break through the clutter and capture the attention of your audience.

The term "message" sounds a bit vague and can actually refer to several related things. Just to be clear going forward, your marketing message includes the following:

- How you talk to the public about yourself and your work
- How you communicate your value to your audience
- How you differentiate yourself from others in the field

Communicating these things in a concise and interesting way is something artists often struggle with. As a listener, it's very painful to listen to someone mumble and blather on with an unfocused, meandering response to a question as basic as, "What do you do?"

As you will discover below, your messaging is presented in so many different areas that it only makes sense to put the effort in up front, so you can implement as needed, rather than trying to reinvent the wheel every time you discover a new outlet.

The number one rule of marketing is this: make your message relevant to your audience. With every communication, you need to answer the fundamental question at the top of every consumer's mind at all times: "Why should I care?" Variations of that question might be, "Is this worth my time and attention?" and "What's in it for me?"

The harsh reality is that people care about themselves far more than they care about you. Even if they think your work is amazing, it's always in the context of how your amazing work is relevant to THEM.

Therefore, before you create your messaging, it's imperative to understand some basic psychology of art buyers, such as their reasons for buying art, what people are responding to, and what themes, topics, or subjects people find relevant. Once you glean these powerful insights, you need to articulate how your work meets the above criteria.

This will help you craft effective messaging that penetrates the wall of indifference and burrows deep into the heart of the art buyer, which is where the majority of purchasing decisions are made. If you connect with their heart, there's a better chance they will connect with your art.

Sell the Benefit

When marketing art, too many people focus solely on the qualities of their creations, virtually ignoring the benefits derived by the potential buyer. While it is important to describe the characteristics, content and intention of the work, it's even more essential to speak to the REASON that people appreciate, support or buy art in the first place. I call this "marketing the Why," instead of merely "marketing the What."

In order to effectively market the "Why," you must understand why people buy art, why they are moved by it, why they choose to actively make it a significant inclusion in their lives. Let's examine some motives for buying art in order to better determine which emotional buttons to aim for when marketing your work:

Beautifying the Home – I've heard the term "couch art" used in a derogatory way to describe certain styles and works of art, but the truth is, creating beauty in one's living space is a common and respectable endeavor. A person's home is their sanctuary, their respite from the hustle-bustle activity of an accelerated lifestyle.

Decorating one's home offers a very personal, singular opportunity to showcase the distinctive styles, tastes and points of view of the inhabitants. Personally, I find it a great honor when a buyer deems my art worthy of being invited into their own personal space, where it will greet them and their guests on a daily basis.

Evoking Feelings – Humans are emotional creatures by nature. Many attempt to maintain a comfortably even emotional keel, avoiding extremes, while others allow the emo-pendulum to swing far and wide so they may experience a full spectrum of sentiments and feelings that authenticate their own existence. Those acutely in tune with their emotions are the ones who love to experience art for the sensory qualities it stimulates.

This describes my friend, Brenda, to a 'T'. She is an artist who creates powerful, visceral, emotionally raw work, and she is drawn to art that moves her in the same way. To Brenda, any movie – from *Ratatouille* to *The Girl with the Dragon Tattoo* – provides an opportunity to shed a tear. Visiting the Seattle Art Museum reduced her to a sobbing wreck, as she was so overwhelmed by the intensity of the creative expression surrounding her. While reading a novel, she vacillates between giddy laughter and sniffling despair.

Art has the ability to affect people in this way. Whether your art excites, relaxes, confounds, inspires or challenges, it will benefit you when marketing your art to know which emotional buttons your work is pushing in the viewer.

Challenging the Intellect – Some people consider art to be a very serious endeavor. The critics, academics and scholars who make up the creative intelligentsia filter artwork through the analytical center of the brain, rather than the emotional center of the heart. Many collectors, curators, museum directors, high-end gallery owners and even fine artists holding bachelor's, master's or doctoral degrees fall into this group as well.

These people can't be bothered with whimsical fluff or derivative dreck. They want their intellect to be stimulated, challenged and surprised by unique and interesting points of view combined with expert craftsmanship. These intellects have studied the history of art and expect relevant artists to be familiar with their own place in the timeline of cultural progress.

If you wish to familiarize yourself with highbrow critical analysis, pick up a copy of *ARTnews* or *Art Forum* magazines. While these particular titles are a bit dry for my taste, it's quite impressive to read the richly detailed, highly academic and smartly considered words, descriptions and critiques by the contributing editors.

If your art makes any type of historical reference, these are the people who expect you to know exactly who, what and why you are referencing. For this group in particular, you must know specifically what you are saying with your work. I mentioned earlier that your marketing message should contain simple language that is easy to understand. I stand by that as a general rule; however, when trying to appeal to the intelligentsia, you must be able to speak their language. Thus, the importance of knowing your ideal audience: who you are speaking to will dictate the level of communication you need to meet them on.

Imparting Status – Some people collect art not for the way it looks in their home, nor the way it makes them feel, nor the emotional or intellectual stimulation, but for the status it imparts. People in this group include serious collectors as well as museums and gallery owners who are interested in the prestige that comes with owning not just a fine art collection, but a rare and distinguished one as well.

This group is interested in works by A-list artists for the cachet big names bring to their collections. They also scout exciting up-and-comers in order to be regarded as trendsetters with their fingers on the pulse of the zeitgeist. This type of buyer is interested in rare, one-of-a-kind or limited-edition works only.

While status-seekers may not be the initial target audience for many of you, it may be a long-term goal for some to show up on their radar at some point in the future. Being recognized by a tastemaker can do wonders for your career, as long as you don't make the mistake of alienating your core audience once you get a taste of the spotlight.

Your Message Starts with Your Name

The first step in creating your marketing message really starts with the name of your business. Let me be clear: if you are making and selling art, you are running a business. Your name is the first thing people hear, so it needs to be catchy, memorable and, ideally, speak to the promise of your offering. In terms of branding, it's best that you pick a business name that will stand the test of time. There's nothing worse than changing names and having to re-educate your public while you re-brand your company.

If you are promoting yourself and your individual works, then it makes sense to simply use your own name. I've had several different company names over the course of my career as I've moved from one discipline to the next, before finally deciding to do all my creative business as Nikolas Allen, LLC. I still remember some great advice I got several years ago from a successful film director who said, "use your given name. Company names change, but your given name will always stay the same." However, there are several other options for you to consider when naming your art business.

Personal Name and Medium/Discipline – The most common practice is using your given name and tacking on your artistic medium. Examples of this would be Brianna Wells Fine Art, Robert Shaw Sculpture, Caitlin Morris Dance Company or Jake Finley Productions.

This approach is not very imaginative, but it is effective. After all, the thing you want people to remember most is your name. You've probably heard the phrase, "build a name for yourself." This means to build up your reputation by having your name attached to the great things you are creating or involved with. Using this naming convention is the most direct route to doing so.

If people are familiar with your work, but not your name, that is a problem. Have you ever had that conversation with someone where you're trying to recall someone's name, and you're furiously describing everything you know about them, while the other person is digging in their memory banks, shouting out random names? You don't want this happening to you.

Some people are fortunate enough to have been christened with great names. If your name happens to be boring, unmemorable or hard to pronounce, you may want to think about using a nickname, or even changing your name.

Nicknames – On the second season of Bravo's reality television show *Work of Art*, there was an artist with the awesome moniker Sucklord, who called his business Sucklord Industries. Now, unless his parents were super freaky—and somewhat sadistic—

this is obviously a nickname. Choosing a name like this is bold, irreverent and memorable, which are all great attributes, but it's also somewhat risky. After all, Sucklord's work never quite lived up to the judges' (or the audience's) expectations and he was eventually booted off the show, proving that his name was all too appropriate.

If you decide to use a nickname, make sure it's unique, easy to spell, memorable, and doesn't have any negative connotations attached to it. Also, be sure to use it consistently across all channels, and not just willy-nilly whenever the mood strikes.

Name Changes – If you decide to go the route of a name change, you should be ready to do it legally and to fully commit to it. I know too many people who make a half-hearted attempt at changing their name, only to flip-flop between birth name and pseudonym, depending on whom they're talking to, which only causes confusion and embarrassment.

Early in my creative career, I was frustrated with my surname. People never quite absorbed it until I spoke it twice and spelled it for them. I knew that would never work if I wanted to be a notorious artist residing in the top-of-mind awareness of my audience. Luckily, my first and middle name created a memorable and pleasing combination to the ear, so all I had to do was legally drop my last name.

I filled out some paperwork, paid a nominal fee, rounded up my brother as a witness, spent a half-hour before a judge in court, and walked out the door as Nikolas Allen. My dad never fully accepted the change and, to this day, still sends Christmas cards addressed to my former self. At least the only confusion caused by this scenario belongs to the occasional mail carrier.

So, if you're concerned about the reaction of your kin or attached to the idea of carrying on the family name for future generations, you may wish to discuss and consider this option long and hard before heading off to court on a whim.

Descriptive Names – An alternative naming option is to use powerful, descriptive words that speak to your artistic discipline, genre or style, and give people a good impression of what they can expect. Examples of this technique might be Yellow Brick Films, Moonstone Jewelry, ContempoArtCreations, Electric Apparel or Acrylix, Inc.

Using this method gives the audience a reference point, which is helpful in our information-saturated society, and offers the opportunity to create something truly memorable. The downside of this is that, no matter how memorable, you're creating a separate entity that is not immediately connected to you. Therefore, you will have to work doubly hard to build awareness of both your company name AND the superstar creative behind the scenes…You!

Combining Both Techniques – Your third option is to use a combination of the two previous options. Examples of this might be Yellow Brick Films by Jake Finley, Moonstone Jewelry by Caitlin Morris, or Brianna Wells' Electric Apparel. The benefit of this is that it serves double duty: it gives the audience a reference point so they have an idea of what to expect, and it attaches your name to the company, which helps to boost your name recognition.

The downside is that this technique usually creates a mouthful that's often difficult to remember. It can also seem as if you're trying to create two brands with this technique, instead of one powerful, memorable one. In many cases, the audience will simply latch on to whatever part of the name is easiest to recall.

CASE STUDY: Authentically Beautiful Photography

Kelly Samuelson is a photographer in Mt. Shasta, California. When she started her business, she decided on the Personal Name + Creative Medium naming technique and, using the first, middle and last initials of her name, she called her business KLS Photography.

When we met, she was already unsatisfied with the name. She noticed that people never remembered the "KLS" acronym (because it's just three random letters that have no meaning to the public) so she started using KLS Photography by Kelly Samuelson.

I told her this was redundant and, if she was going to put her full name in the title, she may as well drop the initials and just call it Kelly Samuelson Photography. However, she was worried about making a big change because she had already invested time and money to promote and utilize the name she had.

She was also worried about confusing and/or losing her current clients with a name change. I told her she was thinking too small, and instead of worrying about appeasing a handful of current clients and hanging on to an utterly forgettable name, she needed to focus on the greater audience that she could attract with a stronger name.

The next time I saw her, she had started using a descriptive tagline under her business name that said, "Authentically Beautiful Photography." I told her that this tagline would make for a stronger company name because it articulated Kelly's meaningful promise, which spoke to the reason people wish to be photographed in the first place. She understood my points, but still wasn't ready to budge.

A few months later, I taught an art-marketing workshop, which Kelly attended. With her permission, I presented a PowerPoint Case Study illustrating her ongoing naming challenges, and spoke about the importance of choosing a meaningful, memorable name for your business.

Within a month of the workshop, Kelly had changed the name of her business to Authentically Beautiful Photography by Kelly Samuelson, an event that was commemorated with a Chamber of Commerce ribbon-cutting that made the newspaper. I feel this is a strong name that speaks to both WHAT is being created, and WHO is creating it. Bravo, Kelly, I wish you much success!

Far too many entrepreneurs take a lazy, uncreative approach to naming their business. This is a shame when you realize that your name is the most important branding element in your marketing arsenal. Your name needs to evoke emotions, visions, feelings, ideas, excitement, expectations, and associations in the minds and hearts of the public every time they hear it.

Keep in mind, it's not just the responsibility of the words for doing this: it's the ideas, actions, ethics and efforts of the person behind the name that hold the true responsibility. So, take the time to choose a great name. Then, take more time making that name stand for something even greater.

Describing Your Work

Whether you are out networking or crafting your promotional materials, you need to be able to explain in great detail the type of art you are creating, why you are pursuing it and how you are executing it. One of the magnificent things about art is that it means different things to different people. However, that does not mean your art "speaks for itself." Artists often trot out this clichéd excuse when asked to speak about their work.

Perhaps they haven't given enough thought to the deeper meaning behind their work. Maybe they are uncomfortable articulating their creative thought process, or they simply fear "giving away all their secrets." Regardless of your apprehension, you must be able to speak for, and about, your art with ease at any given moment. In no way does this mean you have to spill your guts every time someone inquires about your work.

In fact, one of the best replies I've heard at an opening when a patron inquired about the meaning of an artist's work is, "What does it mean to you?" This offers an opportunity to engage your audience and hear directly what their thoughts are about your work. Their replies may even be useful as testimonials or descriptive passages to incorporate into your promotional materials. So, whether you're receiving unsolicited feedback, or directly asking your audience for their thoughts and opinions, make sure you are listening to their answers!

While the evasive approach might work to engage Patty Patron, you may wish to use a different tactic when Cathy Critic is interviewing you for her newspaper article. In this instance, it's essential to be familiar and comfortable with your "talking points" so you come across as engaging, interesting and quotable all at the same time. The point is to know how to comfortably articulate your ideas, your creative process, and your work. Then, how much information you divulge at any given time is up to you and may vary depending on the circumstance.

Three Adjectives – Start by determining three powerful adjectives that describe your work. Have a brainstorming session where you collect all the adjectives that could be used to describe your work. Ask friends and patrons what words they would use to describe it. Break out the thesaurus and find some alternative terms for the common words that show up on your list.

Then, when you've exhausted your possibilities, start editing. Get rid of the weaker ones that don't move you. Ditch the generic words that could be used to describe anybody's work and zero in on the few that elicit a visceral, emotional reaction. Choose the adjectives that paint their own vivid, descriptive picture when uttered, and make certain these pictures are in complete alignment with the art you create.

Talking About Yourself

Because artists spend a lot of time in their own heads, dancing with their creative imagination, many of them tend to be uncomfortable in social situations. To build a successful career, artists must employ an equal mix of online AND offline marketing techniques, which means getting out of the studio and into the public eye.

When out networking, the most common question you will hear is, "So, what do you do?" Unfortunately, 99 per cent of the time that question is asked, the conversation goes something like this:

> "So, what do you do?"
> "Uh, I'm an artist."
> "Oh really, what medium?"
> "Well, lots of 'em really, but lately I've been obsessed with building reclaimed-timber sculptures adorned with carpet scraps, window screens and eggshells."
> "Hmm, sounds interesting. Tell me about these sculptures."
> "Umm, they're kinda like, you know, drawing a parallel between humans and chickens and, like, how our homes are like wombs, and the common practice of nesting, and, um, the need to break free from the shell to emerge into the greater world, and blah, blah, blah…"
> Stifling a yawn, "Excuse me, I think I need another drink."

Instead, you need to formulate a succinct answer to this common question that both explains and intrigues your listener. You do this by creating your **Purpose Statement**. This is a one-sentence statement that explains What you do, for Whom and Why. The structure of this sentence looks like this:

Who / action verb / subject / audience / benefit.

If I were to use this formula to create a Purpose Statement for my art-marketing workshops, it might look something like this:

I / teach / marketing workshops / to ambitious artists / who are ready to gain more exposure.

If I were creating a Purpose Statement for my own artwork, it may sound more like this:

I / produce / provocative pop art / for contemporary urban dwellers / who want to inject their living and work space with a bold, edgy attitude.

When you say this out loud, it may not sound natural at first, but that's okay. You need to craft it, refine it and stick with it. Let's break down the structure of the Purpose Statement and examine the individual points.

The first part, **Who**, is referring to you, so it'll usually be "I," "We" or "My company."

The second part is the **action** you are doing, so it might be "create," "make," "sculpt," "paint," "teach," "explore," etc.

The **subject** is the meat of the statement. It tells your listener what it is your action verb is referring to. This would be a good place to add one or more of your Three Art Adjectives to add a custom punch to the statement that is unique to your work.

The **audience** is who you are making your work for. If you think that "everyone" is your audience, you are mistaken. You need to know who is going to both respond the most to your work, AND derive the most benefit from it. We'll talk more about this later, but to get you thinking in the right direction, examples could be gallery owners, passionate collectors, single homeowners, working mothers, parents of young children, corporate executives, etc.

The **benefit** is the "hook" of your Purpose Statement. This explains the reason why people should care about what you're doing. The minute you realize the benefit your work provides your audience, your marketing message will instantly become more effective. Next time someone compliments your work or says they enjoy it, don't just mumble "thanks": ask them WHY they like it. Try to determine what it is they are responding to. Understanding people's motives for buying art offers valuable insight that will help you better articulate your benefit and improve your message.

The idea here is to create a Purpose Statement that hits all these points so you begin thinking about how to effectively describe your work, your audience and your benefit, and get comfortable talking about yourself in this way. I guarantee the results will be a lot more intriguing than simply stating, "I'm an artist."

The Detailed Follow-Up Answer – The beauty of a concise Purpose Statement is that it weeds out people who are simply attempting to make polite small talk. Some people will be satisfied with just your Purpose Statement, while others will be intrigued and wish to know more. For them, you want craft a detailed follow-up that goes deeper into the meaning, materials, or technique of your art. While you still want to keep it focused and avoid rambling, your detailed follow-up can further explore some of the how's, what's and why's behind you and your work.

By the way, here's an important networking tip: don't dominate the conversation. Sure, people are asking about you, so field their questions in concise and interesting sentences, but don't forget to take some interest in the person asking as well.

It will be a far more engaging conversation if it's not just one-sided, AND by learning about the people who are responding to your work, you are able to build a better profile of your ideal audience. Think of it as a game of tennis, where you lob the attention of the conversation back and forth, and make an attempt to be just as interested in their lives as they are in yours.

1.2

Holding Their Attention

Once you have crafted an intriguing Purpose Statement, and succinct detailed follow-up, this can become the basis of your messaging. You can implement these talking points as needed, which is a lot more efficient and effective than grasping for new words and descriptions every time you need to communicate what you're doing and why it's relevant.

Here are a couple of additional techniques to utilize when addressing the subject of YOU that will maximize the interest and engagement of your audience:

Sell Your Unique Value

Whether you are talking about yourself while networking or being interviewed, or writing about yourself in your marketing materials, you need to be able to articulate what makes you unique as an individual. Sure, this can be uncomfortable to consider, especially for humble people who don't care to spend much time in the spotlight. But if you want to stand out in a world that's completely over-saturated with creative wannabes all clamoring for attention, you need to find your own unique hook to hang your hat on.

Unfortunately, talent alone is not enough. It may have been at one time, but these days technology has leveled the playing field so everyone with a dream now has the capabilities and the tools to reach incredible amounts of people. This means it takes even more effort, thought and creativity to produce messages and content that will stand out among all the noise.

When attempting to define and articulate your unique value, start by asking yourself some questions, such as:

- What adjectives would people use to describe you?
- What life experiences have altered your views and actions?
- What motivates and inspires you?
- What are you passionate about?
- What do you have strong opinions about?
- What are some of your hobbies?

For further personal insights, you may also look to your art. After all, the art you produce says a lot about who you are as a person. Works of art that are deep, innovative or provocative often reflect similar attributes in the artist who created them. The opposite is true as well, which does not bode well for artists who are creating flat, dull, uninspiring works of art.

You can even ask your friends or family. Let them know you are working on your promotional messaging and would appreciate any feedback they may have on you or your art. If they are embarrassed to tell you in person, ask them to write it in an email as if they were answering an inquiry from an art critic, a journalist, or a gallery rep.

Storytelling

Another way to create deeper engagement with your messaging is by telling stories. Storytelling has been a rich tradition throughout the ages. It brings people together, providing entertainment and helping to forge bonds and spread ideas. The art of storytelling has not only spawned the entire entertainment industry, but permeates the advertising industry as well.

Anytime we get lost in a book, a movie, a play, a television show, YouTube video or even a good 30-second commercial, we are allowing ourselves to be mesmerized by the transformative power of storytelling.

1983 was the year my family split up. My four brothers and I were living with our mom in Houston, Texas. She had just separated from her second husband, and was planning our sixth move in as many years. My three younger brothers were sent to live with our father back in Minnesota, while my older brother and I moved with our mom to Santa Fe, New Mexico. I was a shy, overweight freshman in high school struggling to adapt to the culture shock of my new surroundings.

Since I was the "new guy" (yet again) at school, I kept to myself and spent most of my time in class drawing, which allowed me to escape into my own mind. One day, my Religion teacher kept me after class. She said it was obvious that I cared more about art than I did the subject she was teaching. But, instead of trying to punish me, she asked if I would prefer to paint on her wall during class instead of doing the assignments. Of course I said "Yes!"

So, for the rest of the year, while the other students were slogging through their assignments, I was up on a ladder, painting colorful scenes, imagery and religious icons above the blackboard for future students to enjoy. This broke the ice with my classmates, and we started to bond over art, ideas and creativity. Once I started to make new friends, I realized that life in this new town was going to be okay after all.

When working on your Messaging, dare to go beyond the typical stats, facts and figures, and infuse your marketing materials with stories from your own life experiences. This will offer deeper insights into who you are and where you're coming from, which allows for a more genuine connection with your audience.

Your Message Applies to All Channels

Once you refine your message to the point where you have a strong Purpose Statement, you're comfortable talking about yourself and your work, you've got some good stories to share and you are familiar with the type of person buying your style of work and why, you need to think about how all these things apply to the channels you will utilize to get your message out to the public.

We'll be exploring in greater detail the various tools you will implement in Part III, The Right Tools, but to give you an idea of how all the previously discussed elements might be utilized, let's look at some of the places your message might show up:

- Artist's Packet (Cover Letter, Bio, Statement, Image Descriptions, Reviews and Show Announcements)
- Press Releases
- Email Marketing Subject Lines
- E-newsletters
- Email Signatures
- Advertising Headlines, Taglines and Body Copy
- Verbal Discussions
- Printed Collateral (Business Cards, Invites, Brochures, Posters, Postcards)
- Social Media Content
- Website
- Requests to visit your site or follow on Social Media
- Networking

As you can see there are many opportunities to communicate your unique and meaningful message to your audience. While the myriad outlets may seem a bit overwhelming, it becomes a lot easier once you've created a strong messaging foundation that you can pull from whenever the need arises.

This allows you to be efficient with your implementation while maintaining consistency across all your channels, which will help you build a solid, professional reputation as you target your Ideal Audience over and over on your way to achieving success in your creative career.

Speaking of your Ideal Audience, do you know who that is? Let us move on together and discover who you will be targeting with your Right Message.

 **Download the free DTSA Workbook to create your own custom art-marketing strategy:**

www.DeathToTheStarvingArtist.com/workbook

PART II
THE RIGHT AUDIENCE

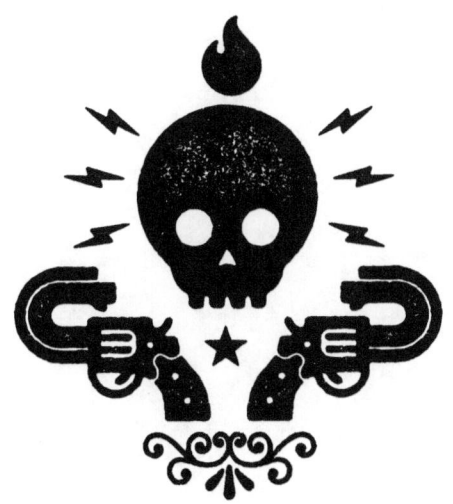

2.1

Marketing to Individuals

When I am teaching workshops, I often ask attendees, "How many of you have sold your work to individuals at some point in time?" Quite often, many hands go up. However, when I ask my follow-up question, "How many of you have all their contact info in a database and keep in touch with them at regular intervals?" there are usually far fewer hands raised.

The best place to start your marketing efforts is right where you are. If someone has bought work from you in the past, they could very well do so again in the future. Therefore, you must collect all the data you can on your previous customers and start building a database that will be the foundation of your initial marketing efforts.

We'll be talking more about the tools you can utilize to reach out to your database in the next section, but for now you want to start looking for patterns or similarities in your current customers that will help you build an Ideal Customer Profile. The more detailed your profile, the more valuable it will prove to be when determining where to focus your future marketing initiatives.

Demographics

Taking note of the physical attributes of your customers will help you determine your target demographic. No, this doesn't mean their physical appearance, but rather the outward evidence of who they are, such as:

Age – The age of your audience will dictate what tone you take with your marketing message. Is it edgy and youthful, casual yet intelligent, or elegant and sophisticated? There are plenty of other tones you can adopt, and noting the age of your buyers will be a helpful place to start when determining your Ideal Audience so you can communicate in a way that resonates with them.

When I launched my Renegade Girl line of graphic apparel in 2007, I was targeting women in their mid-teens to early 20s. Much to my surprise, there were 12-year-old girls responding to it, and there were 50-year-old women responding to it. I had paying customers in every age bracket (pre-teen, teens, 20s, 30s, 40s, 50s; heck, I even got my 60+ mom into a couple of the pieces).

However, even though the age range proved to be wider than I expected, I still created a brand that TARGETED the teens-to-20s woman. If I tried to target the all-ages range, my message would have become muddled, confusing and ineffective. In this case, I found the common unifier wasn't so much age as it was youthful attitude (those who identified with a fun, cute, edgy, playful brand).

Determining the general age range of your Ideal Audience doesn't mean people outside of that range won't respond to your work; it just means that your area of focus is within that range. Then, if different age groups do respond, that's an added bonus.

Gender – Are the majority of your customers men or women? Some art resonates more with one gender than another. Perhaps this is due to the themes addressed in the work, or the point of view, the style, the materials, the color choices, etc. Other work is more universal and offers a wider appeal. The idea is not to have a battle of the sexes mentality, but to take note of who is responding to your work.

When it comes to the people who respond positively to my contemporary pop art, it is a balanced mix of men and women. However, for whatever reason, the majority of my sales have been to women. This knowledge is helpful because if I want to increase my sales in the future, I have a better idea of whom to target with my marketing.

Even as I write this, I can feel some of you bristling at this concept. Now would be a good time to remind you that the reason we bother to consider any of the ideas in this book is so we can generate income doing what we love, which is creating art. However, an art career is not just about creating your art: it's also about selling your art. No sales, no career. Accept that you may have some conflicted feelings about the whole idea of marketing your work, then push through those feelings and keep moving.

Marital Status – Do you create art that would make a swingin' bachelor pad even more swank? Does your art make a young professional's first apartment feel even more like a home? Is your art colorful, fun and whimsical enough to liven up a family room?

When you first start selling your art, there's a bit of a magic bond between you and your buyer. They are taking home a little piece of your creative expression and you want to make sure they will give it a good home. Engaging your buyers in conversation allows you to get more familiar with who they are and what's important in their lives. Are they single, married, divorced? Do they have kids? Sure, these are personal topics, but when you get beyond the superficial, down to what I call the "stuff that matters," your buyers become more than just "customers," but real people with whom you can find commonalities and similar points of interest.

Truthfully, this is what marketing is all about: building relationships with your audience and providing value based on their specific needs, wants and desires. The more you know them as individuals, the easier this is to do. As your business grows and you are showing and selling in more places, this becomes harder to do, but it is worth making the effort when you can.

Education – Smart people and ignorant people both share something in common: neither group wants to feel like you're talking down to them. Smart people don't want you to insult their intelligence and ignorant people don't want you condescending to them. Knowing the educational level of your audience allows you to meet them on common ground and speak a language they are familiar with, which will optimize your communications.

I've often heard people say, "I don't know anything about art, but I know what I like." Of course, this doesn't automatically make them ignorant; it simply means they lack formal education in art theory or art history. These are not the people to try to impress with your extensive art school knowledge. Instead, you converse with them in layman's terms about the visual or emotional aspects of the work, rather than the technical details that went into creating it.

If, on the other hand, you're dealing with an erudite art critic, or a degreed gallery curator, you want to up the ante a bit. In this case, you may wish to demonstrate a little more of your expertise, while still showcasing your unique, winning personality. It's always stimulating to have a conversation that exercises your intellectual muscles, and engaging in this manner will surely leave the other person with a positive, memorable impression. However, beware of pretense. There's a fine line between naturally meeting someone at their level of communication and trying too hard to impress them.

Occupation – What do your buyers do for a living? This is vital information for a couple of reasons. First, your target audience needs to be able to afford your work! Before I started my marketing company, BAM! Small Biz Consulting, it existed in a slightly different form as Art Brand Plan. Back then, my target audience was artists—or Ambitious Creatives, as I like to call them—and my goal was to help artists craft their message and create marketing strategies to help them reach a wider audience. However, my business plan was flawed because most artists can't afford to hire personal marketing consultants! That may sound insulting, but I certainly found it to be true.

I tweaked my strategy to target small business owners, who are typically more willing and able to spend money on growing their business. However, since I am still passionate about the business of art, I do still work with artists. Only this time, I employ tools that will maximize my reach, while keeping the price affordable. This includes teaching art-marketing workshops in group settings and even publishing this book, both of which I pack with practical information for artists who are ready to improve their marketing efforts and grow their business with effective strategies.

The key takeaway here: your audience needs to be able to afford what you're offering. If they can't, go after a different audience!

Secondly, your buyer's occupation may open up further doors of opportunity. An obvious example would be an interior designer. Perhaps this designer buys a piece of yours for her own home, but as you keep in contact with regular communication you might pitch the idea of her keeping you in mind as she works with her clients. Over time, she might find perfect homes for some of your other pieces as well.

What if your buyer is a dentist, or a chiropractor, or a yoga instructor? Perhaps your beautiful, serene works of art prove to be perfect for their office, waiting room or studio. This benefits you by gaining exposure with their clients, and it could also point to a niche market that you hadn't considered targeting. If your buyer's clients are responding favorably to your work (and you know because you are initiating regular communication with your buyers, right?), perhaps you decide to advertise in medical trade magazines, at chiropractic conventions, or in *Yoga Journal*. Always be looking for further opportunity beyond the initial sale.

Psychographics

If a person's physical characteristics identify their demographic, then their mental or emotional characteristics comprise their psychographics. When creating a marketing plan, many people—artists and business owners alike—won't go so far as to include psychographics of their target audience. You can still create an effective marketing plan without this information, but psychographics are often key drivers in many purchasing decisions. Therefore, taking the time to explore them will provide an added layer of depth to your target audience profile that will really help you craft a compelling marketing message when selling your art.

Values – You can tell a lot about a person by their principles, the standards they uphold and what they deem important in their lives. These are their values, and whether you're looking for a life partner, a group of friends or an audience to target with your marketing efforts, ideally you want to seek out people with whom you share similar values.

There was a woman in one of my art-marketing workshops who described her work as "uplifting Christian art." Therefore, when she seeks out exhibiting venues, galleries, art fairs, buyers, or patrons as she moves toward her objectives, she's going to want to target those who identify with and share these Christian values. It will optimize her chances of connecting with her audience if they are familiar (and comfortable) with the religious stories, symbolism and messages in her work.

Desires – If you think about some of the reasons people buy art that we examined earlier in the book, you can identify some of the common desires of your audience. Remember the Homeowner? She desired art that made her home beautiful, that provided a sense of relaxing calm when she returned from a busy day at the office. The Status Seeker, on the other hand, desired the envy of his peers and colleagues, amassing a one-of-a-kind, world-class art collection—regardless of cost.

Then there's the Everyday Art Lover. She's not a rich executive, nor a big name collector, but she has good taste in art, enjoys supporting artists and is slowly building a diverse collection. However, she is on a restricted budget, which means she usually purchases smaller pieces, or saves up over time to buy the "anchor pieces" of her collection. Therefore, she desires distinctive art that speaks to her individual tastes, AND is also priced within her range.

People often have strong feelings of wanting to have something or wishing for something to happen. If you know the desires of your audience, you can speak directly to these feelings and position your art in a way that will inspire people to act upon their desires.

Fears – While I was employed by Liberty Arts Gallery, I heard many comments from patrons who feared they were getting too old because they didn't "get" some of the art. Everybody wants to feel like they're relevant, important or culturally savvy, and feeling like you've been left behind by society, technology or culture can certainly be frightening.

This doesn't just apply to aging art patrons; it could also apply to the Status Seeker who fears losing his clout in the eyes of those who hold him in high esteem. The Important Art Critic might fear becoming passé in a world where everyone with a smartphone and an internet connection can share their opinions with the world in real time. Perhaps the Celebrated Gallery Owner fears the time when the spotlight moves away from her and over to the hot, new edgy gallery uptown that's building quite the buzz.

You see the Fear Strategy used in a lot in non-art marketing by companies that sell things such as tires, plastic surgery, alarm installation and insurance. There's an annoying Yahoo! banner ad for life insurance that I see all the time showing a despondent kid crouching near a gravestone, with a headline screaming, "Who's going to look after your kids when you die?"

Now, hopefully you will never resort to such maudlin marketing techniques, but there is a certain power in knowing exactly what it is that your audience fears. Whether you choose to exploit that fear or not is totally up to you.

Goals – On a more positive note, it's also helpful to know what members of your audience are trying to achieve. We talked earlier about setting your own goals for your art career, so you understand that there are certain factors involved that determine whether you achieve them or not. Often times, people require help to facilitate their objectives.

Knowing the goals of your audience allows you to communicate the features and benefits of your work that might help them meet their objective. To understand what that might mean, we only have to look again at the personality types we've been discussing.

If you are targeting the Everyday Art Lover, whose goal is to build a distinctive collection on a budget, you speak to the beautifully unique statement your art makes, while touting your desire to make your work accessible by keeping price points reasonable or offering payment plans.

If you're targeting the Interior Designer whose goal is to create the go-to brand for über-chic opulence, you want to convey the deliciously rich texture and materials in your work, the sumptuous splendor of your presentation, and your artwork's uncanny ability to effortlessly enhance even the most lavish environs. Play it up, have fun, be bold, be fearless, get outside of your own head and learn to see the beauty and the benefits of your art through the eyes of your viewers, whoever they may be.

Some of this psychographic information may be easier to glean than the rest, but the more you know about your customers, the better you can understand your target audience. This will help you to empathize with them and engage them with meaningful communication that is relevant to their lifestyles.

Remember, you're not just opening up your studio doors, shouting, "Art for sale! Come buy my awesome art!" Instead, successful art marketing requires actively building two-way relationships with your audience. You want to determine who they are, where they are, how you can reach them, and most importantly, how you can deliver value to their lives through your art.

Marketing to Organizations

In the previous section we focused on the different individuals and personality types you may be targeting with your art-marketing efforts. When marketing to individuals, your objective is usually to get them interested in buying your work. When targeting venues and organizations, your objective is usually to get your work accepted into exhibits, shows and fairs.

I will still refer to this as marketing because the same strategic rules apply. These rules include: knowing your work and how to discuss it, knowing your audience and how to reach them, and knowing the benefit and value that your audience will derive from your work. It will also be helpful to consider the personality types we previously spoke of, because they may very well apply to the gatekeepers, curators and employees you will come across when marketing and submitting art to your target organizations.

Choosing Target Cities

You need to determine which cities you will target with your art marketing. In the Objectives Section, we talked about making a plan and I mentioned the pros, cons and best practices of shipping, traveling and exhibiting in different geographic locations. Be sure to consider the information and decisions you made when you were plotting your objectives, and use that as a guide when you start thinking about your target cities.

Just because there are many "great art cities" in the world doesn't necessarily mean they are all right for you, or that you should be targeting them all. Be methodical, be selective, and understand where you are in your career in relation to what feels logical as to where you should be showing your work. In the Right Tools section, we will go into detail about putting together your complete Artist's Packet. In this section, we are focused mainly on where you will be submitting your work.

Start Local – The journey of a thousand miles begins with a single step, and that single step should start right where you are. Where you live may be far from a cultural mecca, but there will still be art opportunities available to you.

I moved away from Minneapolis in 2008 and tried to get settled in San Francisco. When things didn't pan out there, I headed north to Siskiyou County, which includes several struggling little towns up near the Oregon border, including Mt. Shasta where I live, all of which rely on tourism to fuel the economy. My first thought was, "My art career is finished," but I was wrong.

I connected with the Siskiyou Arts Council and volunteered to help curate shows, hang shows, and choose exhibit themes. This led to getting hired to design their show postcards, mentor high-school poetry students, produce poetry slams and teach art-marketing workshops. During this time, my art was also accepted into many of the exhibits at the SAC Gallery, which earned exposure that led to getting into exhibits in galleries throughout the county. Eventually I was hired as Marketing Director at Liberty Arts Gallery, where I curated several exhibits, hung dozens of shows and displayed artwork in many exhibits.

After showing throughout Siskiyou County, I headed north to show in Ashland, Oregon, south to Redding, California, and west to the quaint little town of Weaverville, which has a surprisingly vital art scene. I've also started showing in group shows in San Francisco again, and I'll be investigating the Los Angeles art scene in the near future. The point is, there are probably more art opportunities right under your nose than you realize, so start locally and grow organically according to your planned goals and objectives.

If you are in the early stages of your career, it makes sense to start local, because it takes time to gain experience with the proper preparation, presentation and execution of an exhibit. Even if you only have one piece in a group show, you want to make sure your piece arrives presentable, ready to hang, thoughtfully titled and comfortably priced.

While curating and hanging exhibits at both Siskiyou Arts Council Gallery and Liberty Arts Gallery, I've seen too many pieces submitted that are just not ready to be shown, due to terrible framing choices, poor matting execution, or missing or subpar hanging mechanisms. Many of the artists submitting work simply need a little more education and practice before their pieces are ready for prime time.

Take note of the galleries and creative opportunities in your area. Attend the events, frequent the galleries, meet the gatekeepers, become familiar with what is happening in your vicinity and, even more importantly, where you feel your creative contributions would fit. Start collecting the names, addresses and contact info of decision-makers to target with your inquiries, artist packet and submissions. Then take action!

Grow to Regional – Once you feel like you've explored your own back yard enough, it's time to start looking for opportunities a little further out. Perhaps it's a surrounding town or city, perhaps it's the closest major metropolitan area to where you live, or maybe it's even a state or two over. Whenever you're on road trips, business trips or vacations, be on the lookout for hot cultural pockets, vibrant art scenes and buzz-worthy galleries, and treat your travels as reconnaissance missions to gather all the info that will allow you to properly target these places when you return home.

Then, when you do get home, take action! Build a database of your new contacts, connect with them via social media, join their mailing lists, communicate with them, frequent their websites to keep up with what's happening in their area and seek out opportunities to submit your work.

Aspire to National – Use the internet to explore the art scenes in the major cities. Visit websites of galleries, arts councils and cooperatives, and join the mailing lists of the places that look like they might offer a good fit with what you're doing. While there are numerous galleries, they each have their own niche, focus, mission and genre that they specialize in. Therefore, not every gallery will be a potential target for you. That is a good thing, because it narrows your choices.

It's better to know your own specialty, style, genre, or area of focus and target the organizations that are in alignment with that, than to take a machine-gun approach, spraying submissions at every gallery across the board and hoping you hit a target or two. Besides, there are usually submission fees, which is another reason to be selective: you don't want to go broke just trying to get your work into an exhibit!

Once you start receiving email correspondence from the lists you join, keep an eye out for Artist Submission opportunities that speak to the work you are doing and start submitting. If an organization, such as an art council, doesn't offer an email list but instead regularly posts artist opportunities on their site, bookmark the site and schedule one day per month to hunt and gather submission opportunities.

Consider International – The further you get away from your home base, the more costly it becomes to exhibit your work. Hopefully, you offset the cost in art sales, but that's not always guaranteed. If you are considering targeting an international art market, the process is similar to what we've been discussing above: Discover, Connect, Inquire, Submit. However, sending your art across the world entails different considerations than sending it across the country. Personally, I have not exhibited overseas, so I decided to talk to someone who has.

Christina Z. Anderson is a fine art photographer residing in Bozeman, Montana. She is also an Associate Professor of the School of Film and Photography at Montana State University. I asked her to share some tips and insights based on her international exhibition experience, and here is what Christina had to say:

International Exhibition—Not for the Faint of Heart

Being able to declare on your resume or curriculum vitae that you have exhibited "nationally and internationally" in 100 exhibitions is a wonderful thing. For those of us in the academic field, an international reputation is expected for promotion and tenure. But how to do this on an academic salary without taking out a homeowner's loan is the question. I am a photographer, not a painter or a sculptor, and of these three genres, photography is the easiest to ship overseas. It is flat, can be somewhat reduced in size, and if you are lucky, the exhibition venue will sometimes offer to frame the work and even mat it. This allows you to send flat, lightweight, loose prints.

Here are some tips to consider:

Tip 1: Unless you are Jackson Pollock, many show venues expect you to ship to and from at your own expense, along with the sometimes pricey entry fee.

Tip 2: If you send matted photographs, which are to be framed overseas, the metric system is used. They will cut your mats to fit their frames ever so slightly—a millimeter here or there—and when the prints are returned, they will not fit in your standard American frame sizes. And they'll do all this without telling you. Try to send unmatted work.

Tip 3: Your artwork is to be valued at $0. Yes, you are worthless. Shocking to say, but any value over, say, $50, automatically puts the box into some Customs Purgatory and the work either never shows up, or your international exhibitor has to go down to the customs station and pay to import it. Even worse, you and the exhibitor don't know this and the work is sent back to you with an "Undelivered" label at your expense. Write "$0" in the value field and "For Exhibition Only" in big letters somewhere on the custom form.

Tip 4: The work will somehow return to you on a slow boat from China, no matter where it was exhibited.

Tip 5: Speaking of China, they are very digital-friendly and will actually print out the digital files for you, mat and frame your images, so you don't have to pay for shipping! The only risk here is your artwork may become a screensaver on a million desktop computers.

Tip 6: To keep a sense of humor about all the money you are spending to accrue international acclaim, keep tabs on entry fees and shipping costs for each show line on your resume. Tally up your net worth in expenses, then delete that ol' minus sign, because you and I both know that being able to say on Facebook, "If you happen to be in Ping Yao, China, in March, please visit my exhibition" is priceless.

To learn more about Christina Z. Anderson and her work, visit www.christinaZanderson.com.

Choosing Target Venues

There's a hierarchy of exhibit spaces, to which you will need to gain entry at the start of your career and work your way upward. Quite frankly, there are so many places exhibiting art these days that getting your work shown is not as challenging as getting your work into the right exhibition space that will help move you towards your goals.

Therefore, you want to be both selective and realistic at the same time. Getting accepted into shows is exciting, and it's great for making connections, expanding your biography and making new connections. However, as you progress, you need to be sure you are making vertical strides and not just lateral ones. Let's take a look at the variety of venues available to target with your art-marketing efforts.

Nontraditional Venues

There are numerous spaces and opportunities available to exhibit and sell your work. Again, it's essential to know your objectives so you can gauge each opportunity by its compatibility with your overall plan. If you consider your art career to be like a giant ladder, realize that every artist starts on the first rung and works their way up.

In the following list of exhibition spaces, the venues listed first occupy the first few rungs of the Career Ladder. This is usually where beginners cut their teeth. As you progress through the list, you'll find the more prestigious venues existing on the higher rungs of the ladder. Your goal is to make your way towards the top as you attempt to reach your own version of success.

So, gear up and let's start climbing!

Coffee Shops – Most coffee shops feature art these days. Some place more of a focus on it than others and have rotating works by local artists. While much of the coffee-shop art I've seen has been pretty unremarkable, there have been several times I've been struck by art discovered in coffee shops. In Santa Cruz, I saw some exciting, large-scale, street-art-style work at a hip local coffee joint that made my visit quite memorable.

There's a Yak's Coffee in Redding, California, that hired regional artist Dylan Tellesen to paint a mural on the entire interior of the store, and it's the most awesome and inspiring art I've ever seen in a retail space. While the mural is obviously not for sale, it provided an excellent portfolio piece—and paid gig—for the artist.

Speaking of sales, there's a coffee shop in Benicia, California, featuring adorable small works of art that have a Japanese anime flavor and were created by the owner of the shop. My girlfriend and I noticed the art while on vacation; she followed up with a visit to the artist's website, and finally reached out a couple of weeks later inquiring about a purchase. Even if people love your art, they may not be ready to buy right away. That is one of the many reasons why it's essential to make your art available on the web.

Restaurants – There's a newly opened restaurant in my area of northern California that hired a local arts council vet to curate rotating exhibits featuring local artists. Since I'm friends with the curator, she asked if I would like to exhibit there. Because I'm on a different rung of my Career Ladder, I politely declined, but I know for certain that there are many artists in the area who would love the opportunity.

This is also good example of knowing your market. The restaurant is in an old railroad town that is popular with the fly-fishing crowd. So, even if exhibiting at this restaurant matched my current career objectives, it probably would not be a good place to show my bold, irreverent, contemporary pop art. Remember, you're not just looking for ANY opportunity, you're looking for opportunities that align with your objectives and will help you advance vertically on your Career Ladder.

Wine Bars – There's a popular monthly art walk in Redding that always culminates in a celebration at Vintage Wine Bar. The bar is one of the primary stops on the art walk and features art, live music and vino—three key ingredients of any great art opening. I've also seen some art-centric wine bars in Minneapolis and San Francisco. The atmosphere varies from fun and funky to sleek and sophisticated, and the featured artwork usually follows suit.

On the positive side, wine bars are more upscale than coffee shops, and typically attract a refined clientele, which is great if this is your target demographic. On the downside—and this applies to most of the nontraditional venues—the main purpose of this business is to sell wine, not art. Therefore, no matter how awesome your art is, it often gets relegated to mere décor.

Salons – When I moved to San Francisco in 2008, my first solo show there was at Moxie Salon on Union Street. The salon combined sleek, modern hi-tech with an accessible retro-vintage vibe accentuated by juicy red chairs, a checkerboard floor, and the unmistakable Victorian flair of the building itself. In other words, a perfect match for the colorful glam-opulence of my art. At the time, Moxie was featuring a rotating roster of artists, switching out shows every couple of months, and even holding fun opening receptions. I did sell some work from that show, but the art featured in the salon was clearly of secondary importance to the business of personal beautification. This speaks more to the desires and goals of the salon's clientele than to the efforts of its proprietors.

On the other end of the spectrum is Jungle Red Salon Spa & Gallery in Minneapolis. Befitting its name, this place is more like a punk-rock tiki bar (where I happened to get the best haircut of my life). They have designated an entire third of the space as an art gallery with rotating exhibits. The main difference with this venue is that the owners treat the salon and the gallery as separate entities that coexist in the same space. Instead of feeling like a salon with art on the walls, it feels like a salon with a gallery in the rear quarters. The gallery often hosts art parties, receptions and events, further cementing its status as a cultural hotspot in addition to its reputation as a hot salon/spa destination.

Nightclubs – Many years ago, a new underground dance club was opening in Minneapolis called The Rogue. They held a big grand opening celebration for which they rounded up work by several local artists to showcase throughout the club. This was back when I first started dabbling in visual art, so it seemed like a good opportunity at the time, and I showed several pieces.

In hindsight, it was not even worth the effort, as the art was practically invisible in the dark, loud, gothic environment of the venue. I've seen art displayed in other nightclubs as well over the years, and out of all the nontraditional venues listed here, nightclubs are probably the least likely place people would go to notice, appreciate, or purchase art. So, proceed with caution.

Storefront Windows – Ever since our economy tanked in 2008, there has been an increase in empty storefronts. There's nothing more depressing to visitors than strolling through quaint little cities or towns only to be greeted by numerous desolate, gaping chasms blighting Main Street. The upside of this scenario is that it has given rise to several beautification initiatives that include filling the empty storefronts with work by local artists. There are two towns in my area that have organized full-fledged monthly art walks around these art-filled storefronts. Many of the existing businesses in the area get involved as well, resulting in a beneficial event for the entire community.

As you can see, there are plenty of nontraditional venues available for showing and selling your art, which can be especially helpful at the beginning stage of your career when trying to build your resume. Some of the venues offer better opportunities than others, so be diligent, do your research, and try to choose the right ones to target as you climb the rungs of your Career Ladder. One thing to remember when considering any of the above exhibition opportunities is to make sure your name and contact information (a website is best, as you may not wish to have your phone number on display everywhere) are clearly visible.

If title cards are displayed near your work, the information to include is: Artist Name, Title of Work, Medium, Dimensions and Price. Depending on the venue, you may also wish to have business cards and a mailing list sign-up book readily available to visitors.

Keep in mind, you are not only seeking exposure for your art, but building name recognition as well, while making yourself accessible for sales and further opportunities that may arise from the right people viewing your art.

Artist Co-ops and Associations

They say there is strength in numbers, and artist co-ops and associations offer their members an opportunity to band together and penetrate the art world as a group. This can be a good alternative to forging your path alone, which can be overwhelming and occasionally dispiriting.

Co-ops are essentially galleries run by an organized group of artists. Co-op members pay monthly dues, covering rent and overhead on a communal exhibition space, and they volunteer to work in the gallery space a few hours per month. This guarantees the members a consistent public space in which to stage exhibitions.

The exhibits change every four to six weeks, switching out different work from the same co-op members. This allows you a chance to establish an ongoing presence on the art scene, build a mailing list of interested visitors, patrons and collectors, and sell your art. According to the Mountain Arts Cooperative in

Northern California, "As members, we receive the opportunity to show and sell our art, meet other art lovers, make artist friends, and learn more about the art world."

Associations are similar, but they don't usually operate a gallery the way co-ops do. Members still pay monthly dues and elect a board of directors, but instead of a consistent space, they hold regular board meetings, social gatherings and critiques at various locations and work with existing galleries in order to stage annual (or more frequent) exhibitions.

According to the Siskiyou Artists Association, their mission is to "encourage and foster artist growth, education, development and exposure, while culturally enriching the community."

Joining a co-op or an association can benefit an artist, as it's inspiring and encouraging being amongst a group of comrades with whom you can face your hurdles, forge your plans and celebrate your victories. However, there can also be a downside if the group is plagued by drama, self-interest, inflated egos and conflicting personalities, which creates a toxic environment that can impede your creative progress.

While it can be beneficial in many ways to run with the pack, sometimes it's easier to be a lone wolf. Depending on your personality and your objectives, artist co-ops and associations may or may not be right for you. So, proceed with caution.

Art Fairs and Art Markets

Art fairs and markets are often the unfortunate victim of elitist prejudice. Some artists look upon fairs and markets with disdain, feeling these venues are beneath them, while other artists make a living simply focusing on the art fair circuit. Again, the opportunities you seek need to match your own career goals, and art fairs and markets can be a great way to reach a large audience. However, there are some different considerations involved when doing art fairs and markets than when seeking exhibits at galleries and other nontraditional venues.

Your Display – Art fairs rent out either booths, which are usually minimal skeletons, or space, which is a small, empty, designated plot of ground. Whichever the case, it is your responsibility to determine how to make the best use of the space to display your work. That means you need to determine whether you need tables, portable walls made of wire grids or pegboard, glass or plexi display cases, easels, and racks to display products such as cards, prints, jewelry, clothing, CDs, DVDs, etc.

Make sure you know exactly what is and is not provided at each art fair. Do you need electricity? If so, make sure there is an available outlet near your booth and bring an extension cord (or two) and a multi-plug power strip or adapter. If you show up expecting the organizers to provide you with any of this stuff, you'll be outed as an amateur.

If you choose to go the art fair route, be professional and amass your own portable display equipment that is easy to set up, tear down and transport to different locations.

Weather – Mother Nature is not known for her predictability. Some of the elemental drawbacks to consider with art fairs and markets include the following:

• **Heat** – Are you sitting directly in the sun, or do you have a canopy, umbrella or sombrero to protect you? Either way, better make sure you bring plenty of water and sunscreen. While you're at it, pack a lunch and some snacks. If you're the only one running your booth, it may be difficult to break away to go get food. A hungry artist is a crabby artist, and a crabby artist does not a pleasant merchant make.

- **Wind** – Is your entire booth going to collapse at the first gust of wind? Be prepared with rope, bungee cords, sandbags, tape, Velcro strips and whatever else you need to keep your product in place and ensure that your displays are wind-proof.

- **Rain** – Personally, I like to keep my art as far away from the elements as I can. However, I've seen art fair professionals with their own portable booths who hardly blink an eye when caught in a downpour. They simply zip down the plastic walls, doors and windows to their little art tents and carry on, business as usual. I suppose that's the difference between a weekend warrior and an art fair lifer. If you decide that art fairs are an outlet you wish to pursue, it pays to invest in the proper equipment to keep you and your artwork safe amidst the unpredictability of the elements.

Your Product – Argh, there's the dreaded "P-word"! Yep, if you're producing tangible items to be sold, it is considered product. The key to maximizing product sales and having a successful art fair experience is to understand your audience and their desires.

While art fairs and markets may draw the occasional serious collector—just as garage sales occasionally draw serious antique collectors—they are more likely geared toward the "everyday" art patron, fellow artists and seasonal tourists. Therefore, you want to provide a diverse spectrum of sales opportunities by offering a variety of price points.

Sure, include a few of your expensive, large-scale pieces in your booth, but also include smaller pieces, framed and unframed prints, posters, greeting cards and postcards. Chances are you will sell more of the smaller, affordable, portable works in this environment. If someone responds to your work, you want to be sure you have something that fits their budget, so you don't send them away empty-handed.

Commerce – What type of payments will you accept? If people are paying in cash, you need a calculator to quickly add up their totals, a cashbox filled with plenty of change, and a receipt booklet that you can fill out with each purchase. You may feel nervous, or rushed, but take your time to fill out the receipt completely, which will not only allow you to get your customer's full contact info, but also help you keep track of your inventory and finances. As for taxes, you need to check your local tax laws to see if your products are taxable and how much tax to add to your sales.

> *A Note on Taxes: Depending on how you set up your art business, you might need to get a Federal Tax ID Number (also called EIN, or Employee Identification Number), which is used to identify your business entity. Then you can apply for a Resale License, which allows you to avoid paying sales tax on anything you buy that you will be reselling—like art materials—provided you collect sales tax (which you will report and submit come tax time) from the end buyer when you sell the finished product.*

> *For example, your canvas, paint, eyehooks and hanging wire will be tax-free, because all that goes into the finished product, which you will collect sales tax on when it sells. However, your paintbrushes, palettes, easels and other tools that help facilitate your production will not be tax-free (yes, the merchant will need to ring up two separate sales at the cash register).*

> *Then come tax time, the government will hold you responsible for the tax you did not pay on the supplies, but did collect from your sales. The intricacies of tax laws are beyond the scope of this book, but they become essential once you start making money from your art. When you reach that stage in your career, I suggest seeking advice from a local tax professional.*

As for accepting checks, I would avoid it unless you personally know the customer. It's too easy for a traveler to roll into town, write a rubber check for an expensive piece of art and be five states away by the time you're notified by the bank. You've got far better things to do than chase down fraudsters.

Besides, mobile commerce has become so accessible that there's almost no excuse why you can't accept credit cards. PayPal (paypal.com) is the big player in online payments, but there are several contenders gaining traction in the mobile-payment field. My favorite is Square (squareup.com), which was founded by Jack Dorsey, one of the co-founders of Twitter. You set up an account that is linked to your bank, then Square mails you a free credit card reader that plugs directly into the headphone jack of your smartphone or iPad. People can swipe their cards on the spot, and get a receipt texted or emailed to them.

Square takes a small percentage of each purchase (2.75% as of this writing), and they deposit your money in the bank the following day. So far, the only downside to Square is that the customer "signs" for their purchase with their finger. On the screen. Of your phone. Eww, keep your dirty digits off my iPhone! Ah well, 'tis a small concession to make in order to be able to accept credit cards. However, you may want to invest in plenty of anti-microbial screen cleaners.

As you can see, when it comes to art fairs and markets, there are many things to consider. While some of above considerations may apply to exhibiting in galleries and nontraditional venues as well, art fairs carry a different level of responsibility. Generally, with gallery shows, the curator or staff handles much of the labor and logistics of the exhibit, whereas art fairs require you—the artist—to be the master of your own domain. You are responsible for transporting your work to and from the location, setting up your booth, engaging your audience, handling sales, and being prepared for inclement weather conditions. However, many artists do very well on the art fair circuit, so it's certainly an avenue worth exploring.

Clarify Your Objectives – Art Fairs are condensed into a small time frame, usually taking place over the course of one to three days. Therefore, much like an opening reception, you want to make as many connections as possible in that short amount of time. Knowing your objectives going into the fair will help you make the best use of your time there. In my mind, the artist objective should always include the following:

- Making meaningful connections with new people
- Increasing your visibility and name recognition
- Building your mailing list
- Making sales

I've been to so many art fairs where the artists huddle in their little corner trying to be invisible and, while I understand that many artists are introverted, it is imperative to make a little effort to be outgoing, even if it takes you outside your comfort zone. If visitors express interest, engage them! And don't just make it about you; ask where they're from, how their travels are going, what resonates with them about your art (if you ask this question, listen to the answer! There's nothing more insightful than your viewers describing how THEY see your art).

To build your mailing list, you may simply have a mailing list handy with a written or verbal prompt to join, or you may display a business card receptacle and offer the chance to win a free print to anyone who leaves a card. Then, follow up within a week announcing the winner (we'll talk more about opt-in list-building strategies in the Right Tools section).

With every interaction, and certainly every sale, make sure you exchange your information (on a receipt, sticker, business card, etc.) with their information. If they don't enter to win your giveaway, ask them for a business card and tell them you like to keep in touch with your customers. If they don't have a card, try to get as much of their contact info as possible when filling out their receipt. This may feel pushy to the inexperienced networker, but after several transactions, you will discover the proper wording and a natural flow of information that feels right to you and your customer.

Non-Profit Galleries

The main focus of non-profit art organizations is to enliven the community and enrich the culture through fine art exhibition, education and events. Non-profit galleries are supported by a combination of memberships, donations and grants. While art sales do occur at non-profit galleries, they definitely take a back seat to community enrichment.

The good news for artists is that community-focused galleries offer plenty of opportunities to get involved, to volunteer, to exhibit, even to curate and hang shows. This level of involvement typically does not occur at commercial galleries, making non-profits a great resource and training ground for creative go-getters who are looking to connect with others and make a difference in their communities.

The shows are pretty accessible as well. I've seen exhibits by artists ranging from absolute hobbyists who didn't know to put eyehooks and hanging wire on their canvas, to very successful, late-career artists who still wanted to share their work with the public. I've been heavily involved in two non-profit art spaces for several years and it has offered some of the most rewarding experiences of my creative career.

Commercial Galleries

Once an artist reaches a certain stage in her career, the main focus often shifts to the commercial galleries. These venues are on the higher rungs of your Career Ladder because they are more difficult to get your art into. Unlike the alternative venues, commercial galleries aren't simply out to fill their walls, decorate their space, or provide enjoyable ambiance for their customers. They are out to build a sterling reputation and a successful business by seeking out important talent, fresh voices and exciting works of art with the intent of attracting patrons, art lovers and collectors who aren't just interested in viewing the work, but buying it as well.

Sure, commercial galleries care about enriching the culture, but they are first and foremost running a business, and businesses need revenue in order to survive.

The art business world moves in cycles, and the recent economic crash and ensuing recession have certainly caused a downturn that forced many galleries out of business. The good news is this: there are still plenty of commercial galleries that are alive and kicking, and it's your job to locate them, attract them with your amazing art, and line up exhibit, sales and representation opportunities!

However, just because there are numerous commercial galleries in existence does not mean they are all potential targets. Remember, marketing is not about casting the widest net possible: it's about honing in on the most appropriate prospects and engaging them with your relevant, meaningful message, your unique story and your magnificent art. Therefore, you must be selective.

The first criterion is to find out which galleries are showing work that is similar to yours. If you're starting in your own city or region, maybe you're already familiar with some of the galleries you want to target. Become a regular at those galleries, visit their websites, get to know the staff and get familiar with their exhibition schedule and submission process. Outside of your own area, you want to start your research based on the cities you've already targeted.

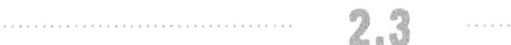

2.3

Seeking Your Targets

Now that you have a better idea of all the different venues providing opportunities to exhibit and sell your art, the million-dollar question is, Where do you start? It helps to honestly assess what rung of your Career Ladder you're currently on. Acknowledge your current level of experience and determine your initial targets accordingly. You can either aim for opportunities that exist on the same level, or you can aim for targets a couple of rungs higher than you currently are. The responses and feedback that you receive will let you know if it's time to elevate your sights, and it will tell you if you are aiming too high.

Keep in mind that you want to progress in an upward trajectory. Lateral is okay for a while, but try not to get too comfortable with easy opportunities. It's best if you continue to challenge yourself. There are many tools you can use for discovering available venues and opportunities. The following list is a good place to start:

Internet Search
The idea is to build a master list, spreadsheet or database of potential venues that you can target with your submissions and inquiries. Keep in mind, when doing any research, Google is your friend. If, for example, you're targeting galleries in Miami, Florida, you can type related keywords and phrases, such as "art galleries miami fla," into your Google search box and scroll through the search results. The more specific you get with your phrases, the more targeted your results will be.

The only punctuation search engines care about is the comma. Adding a comma acts as a break between search terms, which the search engine views as a list of several different items, rather than a complete phrase. In order to turn up relevant results that are narrowly focused, use complete and specific phrases without commas. I repeat, do not use commas in your phrases if you want targeted results. Also, don't worry about capitalization or periods. That stuff is for mere humans, not omniscient internet robots.

By varying the keywords you are searching for, you may get different results, which will help narrow your options according to your niche or specialty. Examples of that might be, "sculpture galleries miami florida" or "art exhibition opportunities miami fla." Also, as you're typing in your search terms, a dropdown list appears offering several suggestions based on common searches. There may be some search terms you haven't thought of, so try some of the ones that seem interesting or appropriate to what you're looking for.

Online Arts Councils

One of my favorite resources when looking for submission opportunities is the California Arts Council (www.cac.ca.gov). They've got an amazing list of artist calls from galleries that you may not have discovered in your own searches. Plus, their updated and extensive list is an easy, one-stop resource offering a qualified selection of legitimate opportunities from people who are actively seeking your work!

So, when searching on Google, don't limit yourself to just galleries. Also look into all the various arts councils and organizations. Considering the search info mentioned in the previous section, you can type in your state name followed by "arts council" and see what comes up. You can also break it down into city or county according to your target region, and again, mix up the order of the search terms, such as "sonoma arts council" vs. "arts council sonoma county." Remember to be selective with the artist calls you do answer. Make sure they are geographically and financially feasible and fit within your career growth plan.

Art Publications

My two favorite art magazines are *Hi-Fructose* and *Juxtapoz*. They focus on contemporary artists creating fresh work that is exciting, inspiring, surreal and, quite often, a bit macabre, which speaks to me both as a reader and an artist. Therefore, the myriad galleries advertising in these magazines are high on my list of targets.

There are several other art titles on the magazine racks of finer bookstores, such as *Art News*, *Blue Canvas*, *Art Forum* and *Art in America*. In addition to the gallery advertisements throughout these publications, there is usually a Classifieds section featuring open calls for submission. Purchase or subscribe to the publications that speak to you as an artist and use them as resources to discover compatible galleries for you to target with your submissions and inquiries.

Referrals

Sometimes, the best way to discover new galleries is by talking with other artists who have been actively exhibiting. Maybe they are further along in their career, or perhaps they are simply living in a different region than you and have some inside information on the scene in their area. This is all the more reason to break out of your comfort zone and make an effort to meet your creative peers, talk shop, and share ideas with other artists. The artist's journey is unique, and it can be isolating as well. It's important to view other artists not strictly as competitors, but also as potential allies.

I was exhibiting at a group show at ARC Gallery in San Francisco and was having a hard time breaking out of my isolated box at the opening reception. It was my first time at that gallery and, aside from my girlfriend who came with me, I didn't know anyone. I finally made the effort to approach a tall man who had been standing in the center of the room wearing a leather jacket, fedora and fashionable eyewear—clearly the uniform of an artist.

Sure enough, we struck up a great conversation. I discovered that we shared the same first name, that he was up from Santa Barbara to exhibit in the show, and that his irreverent, somewhat whimsical sculptures had been starting to garner some attention down south. About halfway through our conversation, he referred me to a woman who owns a gallery in Ventura, California.

When I returned home from the Bay Area, I Googled the reference he gave me and discovered tons of info about this woman and her amazing gallery. She went onto my list of targets and, as it turned out, this was the only lead that came out of my SF exhibit. So, not a super fruitful exhibition experience, but it's a good thing I reached out to at least one of my peers.

Harvesting Contact Information

The whole point of your search is to find compatible galleries and collect contact information so you can send inquiries or submissions that will lead to getting your work into their gallery. Therefore, when you come across galleries of interest, add the pertinent information to your database. Your first stop should be the gallery website, which will usually give you all the information you need to know.

- **Name of Venue**
- **Main Contact Name** – Is there a head curator, or are you sending to the owner? It's always better to address a specific individual, so if no names are listed on the website, consider calling and asking for the name of the person who reviews submissions.
- **Address** – Where is the gallery? Perhaps you divide your database into regions so you can target one region at a time.

- **Email Address and Phone Number** – This should be listed somewhere on the site. In lieu of an email address, some galleries may just provide a contact form, which is a way to reduce the amount of spam they receive. Collect whatever contact info you can glean for your database.

Submitting Your Artist Packet

When submitting your work to galleries, you want your first impression to be a positive one, so be sure to use proper submission etiquette.

Blind Submissions – If you were unemployed and looking for a job, you probably wouldn't send unsolicited resumes to every company you wanted to work for, regardless of whether or not they were hiring. You could, but it wouldn't be the most effective use of your time or resources. Same goes for artists looking for exhibition opportunities.

Different galleries may react in different ways to blind submissions (submitting work when there's not an active Call for Submissions in play). Some may take the time to examine them eagerly with the hopes of discovering raw, fresh talent, while others will not even look at anything they have not specifically and publicly requested.

If you discover an awesome gallery that you feel would be a great fit for your work, and their website doesn't mention anything about public submission opps, call the gallery and ask them about their policy on considering new artists.

Calls for Submissions – Venues that are actively requesting new works are the proverbial low-hanging fruit of the art world. Targeting these places should be where the majority of your time and marketing efforts is spent. Be careful, however, not become so excited by the amazing opportunity that you forget about feasibility and logistics.

Consider where the show will take place, how you will get your work there and back, and whether or not you will attend the reception. Think about the costs involved for the submission fee, as well as the shipping fees if you're accepted, and travel costs that may accrue if you are attending an opening that's out of your area. In other words, consider the whole process—including things we've discussed like target audience and career objectives—before submitting your work. Only submit if you plan to follow through, because you just may be accepted, and that's when the real work begins.

Entry Rules and Guidelines – So, you've considered all of the above and have decided to submit your work. Congratulations! Next thing you need to do is study the rules and guidelines. They will either be sent to you with your acceptance notification, or they will be posted online. Either way, read them and follow them.

Regardless of how much you fancy yourself a rebel, a badass, a contrarian or an anarchist, you must follow these guidelines to a "T" if you want your submission to be considered. If you don't, you're practically begging the curators to reject your submission. You're telling them that you don't respect their rules, and do not care whether you're accepted or not. And, if you want to play the game, you've got to play by the rules, like it or not.

The reason I'm stressing this point is because I have curated many shows and am constantly surprised at the details people overlook, forget or just plain ignore when submitting work. This includes something as important as the deadline! Sorry, you are not a special exception. Get your work in before the deadline or you will not be in the running. Period. Either put your best foot forward every time, or don't bother submitting.

Follow-Up – Usually, somewhere within the Artist Call, the venue will specify a date in the future (generally a month or so after the submission deadline) when they will have decided who has been accepted and who has not. Around that time, they will send out acceptance letters and rejection letters. However, not all galleries send rejection letters. Some rely on silence to communicate the bad news, trusting that if you DON'T hear from them, you'll assume the worst.

If you're the type of artist who really wants closure, it's perfectly acceptable to follow up with the venue and check on the official status of your submission. However, make sure you wait until after the specified "decision date" before calling to inquire. If there is no decision date specified, give it at least three weeks before inquiring. Putting together an exhibit is a lot of work and sometimes takes longer than planned. You don't want to come off as the child in the backseat of the car, kicking Dad's seat while asking, "Are we there yet?" every five minutes.

Take Rejection Gracefully – It can be painful to have your artwork rejected. It's a bruise to the ego and can put a dent in your confidence. While these feelings are natural, you must not let them impede your progress. In regards to your art submission, rejection is not personal, so don't take it personally. There are many reasons your art may not be right for a certain exhibition, and none of them are because the jury wanted to attack or punish you personally.

However, if you raise a ruckus, cause a stink, or generally act like a poor sport, you are giving them a reason to dislike you personally, and THAT will be remembered next time your name comes up or your submission crosses their desk. I've seen artists cop bad attitudes, throw hissy fits and get belligerent when their work is rejected, and it's never endearing. Just remember, you will win some and you will lose some. So, be strong and take rejection like a pro.

Submit to Future Shows – If there is a gallery you really want to exhibit with, and your submission is rejected for a show, don't write them off completely and delete the gallery from your database. Keep your eye on their schedule and submit to future shows that intrigue you. This is another reason why you want to act professionally upon rejection. You don't want to soil your name and reputation by acting a fool, but rather build name recognition as a tenacious artist who perseveres in the face of adversity.

With all the exhibits I've curated, I have seen a lot of the same artists submitting work over and over again. Your work may be accepted for one exhibit and not another, but that shouldn't stop you from submitting to other exhibits in the future.

Some galleries have a specific person or group of people who jury every show, but many galleries have a rotating cast of jurors and guest curators who will bring fresh insights and ideas to each exhibit. Some of these gatekeepers will be lenient with their acceptance policy, adopting an "everybody wins" attitude, and others will be extremely selective, in order to achieve a certain vision. In my opinion, it's better to err on the rigorous side. This challenges artists to submit their best work, both technically and thematically, thereby raising the bar and creating the strongest exhibition possible.

The bottom line is that artists improve and juries rotate. So, don't give up on a particular gallery after one rejection; be persistent with your future submissions.

 **Download the free DTSA Workbook to create your own custom art-marketing strategy:**
www.DeathToTheStarvingArtist.com/workbook

PART III
THE RIGHT TOOLS

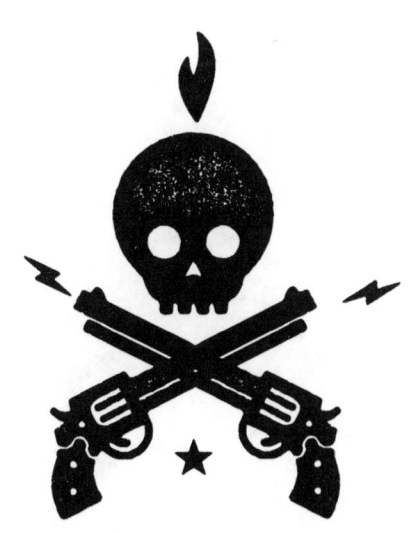

Loading Up the Toolbox

Now that you've crafted your Meaningful Marketing Message and determined your Ideal Audience, it's time to choose the Right Tools to implement in order to reach that Audience with your Message. Whether you are working on a kitchen remodel, tinkering under the hood of your car, or fixing your child's favorite broken toy, the outcome is always more effective when you're using the proper tool for the job. This same philosophy applies to marketing yourself and your art.

There are way more tools available than you can possibly put to use. I will be outlining many of the essential tools in this section, and it will be up to you to determine which tools will fit best into your arsenal in order to meet your objectives. You may be determining your own criteria for choosing which tools to use, such as ease of use, widespread reach or because you're already familiar with the platform.

However, I would like to emphatically state that the best reason to use a certain tool is because it puts your work in front of the Ideal Audience you are trying to reach. Keep that in mind as you're choosing the right tools for the job.

The Essential Artist Packet

These days, it's quite common to submit your work electronically via email or through an online form, where you enter your information into fields and upload JPEG images of your art. In other cases, you will be sending a physical artist packet through the mail. In either scenario, it's important that you have already created your packet ahead of time, so that you can now simply cut and paste as needed for the digital submissions, and duplicate and mail for the physical ones. In other words, try to become efficient with your submissions, and don't waste time trying to reinvent the wheel each time you have to put a new submission together for a different gallery.

Let's look at the different elements you will need to produce for your promotional packet. You may not use all of these all the time, but again, it's best to create them now so you can use them as needed.

Cover Letter – Think of this as your general introduction. If you're sending a blind submission, or there is no active Call for Submissions, you may want to be a little more detailed in your cover letter. Address the person you're trying to reach by name (which you discovered when you were researching your Ideal Audience, right?), and let them know Who you are, How you found them (if you're working off a referral, go ahead and drop names), What you want and Why you think your work would be a good match for the venue.

Your cover letter should end with a call to action. Depending on what your objective is (getting a meeting, getting a show, getting representation, etc.), your call to action may vary, but always end strong and don't leave them guessing what the next step is. Do you want them to call you if they are interested in your work? Are you going to follow up with them with a specified time? Be clear so they can take appropriate action as needed. Also, keep your cover letter short, sweet and to the point, so its recipient can get to the good stuff (your art) quickly.

If you're submitting work via email in response to a Call for Submissions, the body of your email can be considered your cover letter. Again, keep it brief. You might also be required to include titles, sizes, materials and prices of the pieces you're submitting. Include that info in your email and attach your additional files, such as statement, bio, images and whatever else has been requested. Try to submit your whole package as a multi-page PDF or Word document, rather than attaching a bunch of separate documents. When lots of submissions are rolling in, whatever you do to help your recipients with keeping things organized will be appreciated.

If you are submitting work via an online form in response to a Call for Submissions, a cover letter is rarely necessary since the objective is clear and the form usually cuts right to the chase. Just be sure to fill out all the fields with your appropriate information. Double-check all your grammar and spelling before hitting the Submit button. Then, cross your fingers!

No matter how you are submitting your work, always make sure to include your name and contact info in several spots (on your cover letter, in your email, on your attached documents) so someone can get ahold of you quickly if necessary. This seems obvious, but when lots of details, dates and deadlines are involved, it's the obvious things that can slip through the cracks.

Artist Bio – The point of an Artist Bio is to highlight your exhibition record. The term 'bio' can be confusing because it is short for biography, which is defined as "an account of someone's life written by someone else." Considering this definition, you might be tempted to write about yourself and your life as if you were writing an About Page or even an Artist Statement. Instead, think of your bio as your resume.

Some of the topics to include are solo exhibitions, group exhibitions, publications that you were reviewed in, collections your art is in, commissions you have received/produced and pertinent art education. As with all the documents in your Artist Packet, you also want to include a header that includes your name, address, phone number, email and website.

Start with the most recent activity and work your way backwards in reverse chronological order. If you've had solo shows, list those first; otherwise, start with your group exhibitions. If you're truly just starting out and don't have anything to list yet, that's okay: everybody needs to start somewhere.

It may take a while to build a bio that looks impressive, but keep at it and be sure to add to each new activity to your bio as you go, so you're not digging through your memory bank months later trying to remember where and when you've exhibited.

When listing your activities, whether exhibitions, publications or education, the format should be consistent. Here's how it should look:

Selected Solo Exhibitions
Gallery Name, "Exhibition Title," City, State, Month, Year

Selected Publications
Publication Title, "Article Title," Month, Year

Education
Degree or Subject, School Name, Year

When it comes to your bio, "Your career should look vigorous and professional," says Cay Lang, author of art-business book *Taking the Leap*. "It should indicate that you take a responsible and dedicated attitude toward your art, that you are committed for the long term, and that your art is vital and in demand."

Artist Statement – Your Statement needs to describe what it is that you are "saying" with your art. If there are certain topics or issues that are important to you and making their way into your art, this is where you discuss them. There aren't many original ideas left in the world, but there are a million points of view. Your Artist Statement is where you explain your creative point of view.

Many artists find it difficult to talk about their work. They feel they shouldn't have to "explain" it: they want viewers to form their own interpretations, or they think their art should "speak for itself." Regardless of whether you choose to explain your work or not, you should still be able to verbally communicate the ideas, concepts and viewpoints utilized in your art.

You will also describe what techniques, medium and materials you are using and why. I know an artist who creates works using only discarded garbage, junk and litter that she finds on the ground, and she is clearly able to articulate her reasons and intentions. Whatever you're working with, you need to be able to say what it is you enjoy, or find challenging, about the process.

When you are writing your Artist Statement (and all the rest of your promo materials for that matter), use simple language that the average person can understand and relate to. Trying to be too academic or esoteric will only make you sound like a pretentious windbag, which will result in your audience tuning out immediately. Leave the art-speak for the critics and simply write from the heart, using your own voice.

Reviews/Testimonials – In traditional marketing, testimonials are a very powerful tool used to convince an audience that a product or service is legitimate and valuable. People tend to place a lot more trust in the opinions of their friends, family or other influential people than they do in marketing materials and advertising copy produced by the company trying to sell their product. Of course, this applies to art as well, which is why viewers and collectors place so much weight on the opinions of critics and tastemakers.

When marketing your own work, you could say how awesome, amazing and innovative your art is, but people will be skeptical and proceed with caution. However, if an art critic, a gallery owner or a respected art blogger says the same thing, it will carry a lot more weight. For this reason, you want to include reviews and testimonials in your Artist Packet. It may take years before your art gets enough notoriety or attention for an art critic or publication to actually review your work, so until then you can use the words of the people in your direct art circle to great effect. That could be the gallery owners who show your work, curators who accepted your work into an exhibit, the art critic at a local newspaper, or even the members of the public who attend your shows.

Don't be afraid to ask a gallery owner to describe your work in her own words, or talk about why she enjoys dealing with you as an artist. Listen to the comments and feedback you get when you're speaking with visitors at an opening reception. When I was making short films and music videos in the aughts, I tended to mix a bright, color-saturated visual aesthetic with darker undertones of content and story. One viewer said that my work "celebrated the soul and its shadow," a quote I thought was brilliant and used generously in my marketing materials.

Of course, you also want to collect any reviews or press mentions that appear in the local media, be it in print or online. The Review/Testimonial page of your Artist Packet may take some time to build, but if you start off with the mindset that you're an aggregator of thoughts, feedback, soundbites, quotes and critiques of your work, you can build this section organically as your career advances.

Keep a physical file in your studio/office where you save all your hard-copy media mentions, as well as a digital file or document on your computer where you type up or cut-and-paste verbal or online mentions. Then, when you feel like you've amassed a decent collection of powerfully persuasive insights and opinions, add this section to your Artist Packet.

Images – The photographs of your artwork need to represent each piece as best they can. All the other marketing work we have covered up to now will do you no good if you don't have high-quality images of your art. If you are savvy with a camera and know your way around a computer, you can shoot your work yourself. If not, hire a friend or a professional to photograph your art. Key points to consider when shooting your art pieces are focus, lighting, composition and image quality. Curators and gallery owners base their decisions on what they see in your photos, so this is not an area you want to skimp on.

Before digital photography came along, slides were the preferred method for viewing an artist's body of work. While some high-end galleries may still request slides (I haven't experienced this, but I'm well aware that some people refuse to change with the times), these days it's really all about the JPEGs (compressed digital photos).

Some of the ways you will be submitting images of your work include uploading them to a gallery website, emailing them to the curator, or sending them on a CD through the mail with the rest of your Artist Packet. The process you want to get comfortable with is shooting digital photos, uploading them to your computer, and resizing them to the optimal size depending on your requirements.

Typically, if you are using your image on the web, it needs to be low-resolution (72dpi) so it loads quickly. That doesn't mean it has to be a tiny, pixelated thumbnail. An image can be large in size (width × height) and still be low-resolution (dots per inch). However, sometimes a gallery will request that you upload or email high-resolution images (300dpi) so they can zoom in on the image and see the quality and detail in your work. That's where the image format comes into play.

I mentioned JPEG earlier, which is a compression format that compresses a hi-res image to a manageable size so it can be uploaded or emailed. The acronym stands for Joint Photographic Experts Group, which is the name of the group of big brains who created the format standard.

If you intend to print your images (on your promotional items, in a newspaper or magazine, or for a physical portfolio), they need to be high-resolution (300dpi). One thing to keep in mind is that you can shrink a hi-res image and make it lo-res, but you can't take a lo-res image and make it hi-res. For that reason, I like to make duplicates and place them in separate folders marked "Hi-Res" and "Lo-Res."

The hi-res images will be used for printing or sending to members of the press, and the lo-res images will be used for emailing or posting anywhere on the web, including your own blog, portfolio sites and any social media platforms. Dealing with digital photography, formats, resolution, pixels and sizes can be quite confusing, and it has taken me years of practice to become familiar with it.

So, the bottom line is that you need one set of high-resolution images and one set of low-resolution images of every piece of art in your collection. Then, use the appropriate image, format and resolution needed to meet the objective at hand. You can usually find a tech-savvy friend, peer or colleague who is willing to help, so don't be afraid to ask when necessary.

SASE – Even though I've been talking about email and websites, we're still talking about building a physical Artist Packet in this section. You should include a Self-Addressed, Stamped Envelope only in the event that you're sending something out that you want back. In the days when people were sending slides out to several galleries at a time, they obviously wanted them mailed back because they were expensive and could be used many times over.

These days, you might be sending out a CD of images, or even a printed portfolio that's bound in a clear, plastic sleeve you get at an office supply store (I have gotten both interest and exhibits by approaching venues with such a thing). While both of these things are cheap and relatively disposable, you may want to get them back to use more than once. If so, get an envelope that will fit the desired item properly and address the envelope to yourself.

Go to the post office and purchase enough postage to cover the return journey. Then, if you're rejected by the gallery, they can drop the desired item in a mailbox and it will come home to you to be used in another submission. If you do not want anything back when you submit your Artist Packet, there is no need to include a SASE.

Cardboard Backer – The U.S. Postal Service is notorious for getting large parcels to fit into small mailboxes. If you don't want your submission packet to arrive at its destination looking like an accordion, slide a stiff piece of cardboard into your envelope before sending. If you are sending a CD of images, you can tape the corners of the CD sleeve to the cardboard so it stays secure during shipping. Just make sure you call attention to its location in your cover letter, so the recipient doesn't pull the contents of the envelope out and leave the cardboard piece behind.

Large Envelope – Once you have created all the items in your Artist Packet, put everything together in a large envelope. Rather than putting together one packet at a time, I like to create a small assembly line and assemble 10–12 packets that are ready to mail as they are needed. Of course, you want to leave the envelopes unsealed until you add the custom items such as the cover letter and mailing address. Then you can scroll down your list of target venues, craft your individual cover letters as needed, address your envelopes, and send. Keep track of your responses and follow up when necessary.

Here is the preferred order of items, from top to bottom of stack, when assembling your Artist Packet:

1) Cover Letter – On top
2) Artist Bio
3) Artist Statement
4) Reviews & Testimonials – Only if you have them
5) Images – CD (or preferred method specified by gallery)
6) SASE – If you want something returned
7) Cardboard Backer – On bottom
8) Large Envelope – Contains everything listed above

3.2

Launching Your Website

"Every freelance artist—writers, painters, musicians, comedians—should plan to be an internet impresario. All artists should understand the basics of money and how to sell their genius, through social networks and every other modern form of communication. Many of the cannier (and perhaps younger) ones are already going it alone. They have organized websites to display their works and formed co-operatives to organize venues to perform and exhibit."

– Luke Johnson, Chairman, Royal Society of Arts

Think of your website as your main online hub. Your art needs to be online and easily accessible to view for curators, gallery owners, collectors and even curious friends and family members who have never quite understood what you do. In the past, websites were cost-prohibitive and if you wanted one, you were beholden to a webmaster who was responsible for every little change or update to your site.

Technology has gotten to the point where websites have become very affordable and easy to maintain if you have a little bit of technical savvy. With cheap hosting plans and user-friendly web platforms like WordPress, building and maintaining your own site has become a lot more feasible. Even if you decide not to do it yourself, more people have become proficient at using site-building tools like WordPress, so it is easier and cheaper than ever to find someone to help you with your site.

Master Your Domain

Whether you're building your own site, or hiring someone to build it for you, the first step to creating your online property is to claim your domain name. Typically, your website domain name will be the same as your art business name, so the first step is to see if your desired domain name is available. There are several online companies that will sell you domain names (see Resources), but GoDaddy is the big kahuna of domain registration, so I suggest starting there.

On the home page of godaddy.com, there's a text field where you can type in your desired name to see if it is available. If it is available, you have two options: You can either go ahead and purchase it through GoDaddy, even if you'll be hosting your site elsewhere (while GoDaddy is great for domain search and registration, I prefer hosting with other companies such as Host Monster or Host Gator), or you can purchase your domain name through the company who will be hosting your site.

Finding a good domain name can be frustrating because many times you will come up with the "perfect" domain name only to find that it is already taken. You know the old saying, "There are no new ideas in art"? Well, the same applies to domain names. No matter how brilliant your domain name is, someone else has probably already thought about it—and purchased it. Even if you are simply using your personal name as your business name, it's not always guaranteed that it will be available as a domain.

If the domain name you want to use is already taken, GoDaddy will offer suggestions for similar names that are available. You can either browse those or come up with your own alternatives, such as tacking "art" "fine art" "sculpture" or any other medium after your name. As for suffixes, there are a whole slew available, such as .biz, .org, .net, .me, but .com (dot com) is the most widely used and the first option people try when looking up anything on the web.

Therefore, unless you are a non-profit organization—in which case you would use dot org (.org)—I would recommend using dot com as your suffix.

Four Attributes of a Good Domain Name:

1) Short – When typing words into a browser, especially on a mobile device, the shorter the better.

2) Memorable – If someone sees your work offline and they are intrigued, you want them to be able to recall your personal or art business name next time they're in front of a computer or mobile device. Therefore, avoid the temptation to get too tricky or clever with your domain name.

3) Easy to read – Since domain names string multiple words together in lowercase letters, viewers have to work a little harder to understand them at a glance. Some words string together better than others, so try to settle on a domain name that reads well and doesn't look like gibberish.

If you settle on a domain name that IS difficult to read in URL form, you can capitalize the first letter of every word on your printed materials (e.g., "Visit me online at MalloryMeyersFineArt. com"), so humans can understand it. Keep in mind that search engines don't follow punctuation and grammatical rules, so don't bother with capital letters when setting up your domain.

4) Descriptive – We talked about crafting descriptive names in the Right Message section. The difference with domain names is that you are not only writing for humans to understand, but also robots (i.e., search engines). There's a lot of talk in the marketing world about using domain names that contain rich keywords that will help with search rankings.

An example of that would be using "fineartsculpturemiami.com" (Fine Art Sculpture Miami), which would show up when someone searched for those terms, instead of using "jensmithsculpture.com" (Jen Smith Sculpture), which may not be as visible in search results for the same keywords.

While keywords are important, I prefer to write for humans rather than robots most of the time. I would rather build a brand based on my art business name than use generic terms that get me found by more people on Google. It depends on your objectives, though, so give it some thought.

Host with the Most

Once you've purchased your domain name, the next step is to purchase a hosting plan. I mentioned a couple of hosting companies above (see Resources for more), so you can investigate those options to see which one feels right for you. Most of the A-list hosting companies are touting the same features, which has reduced hosting to somewhat of a commodity. Things such as unlimited disk space, bandwidth and email accounts, easy cPanel control, and high-percentage of uptime are all pretty standard.

Therefore, you may wish to look for the some of the unique differences touted by each company that are either meaningful or important to you (this is a prime example of the power of differentiating yourself with meaningful messaging).

For example, if you are a proponent of alternative energy, you may choose the company that uses renewable energy sources to power their company (HostPapa and HostGator). If keeping jobs in the U.S.A. is important to you, you might choose the company using 100% U.S.-based support teams rather than outsourcing jobs overseas (HostMonster).

If you feel strongly about animal rights issues—or, conversely, if you're an avid hunter—seeing the company CEO post photos online of himself standing over a dead elephant during his latest safari hunting expedition (GoDaddy) might play into your decision as to where you put your money when it comes time to invest in hosting.

In my mind, the most important factor is 24/7/365 technical support. Not only do you want to be able to contact support whenever you need to, you also want it to be a pleasant experience. When you are stressed out or confused about technical problems, you want to feel like you're speaking with someone who cares about you and your site. Since customer service depends on the mood and personality of the individual you are dealing with, it can be inconsistent unless the company mission includes a service-oriented culture.

This is where positive referrals from your own circle of influence can come in handy. When determining which hosting company you will go with, ask around for feedback from people who already have their own website. Listen for positive and negative stories regarding their web-hosting issues or tech-support experiences.

When you do finally make your decision on which company to host your site, you have the option to sign up for short-term or long-term hosting. If you're unsure about the company and want to try it out, purchase the one-year option. Once you have found a company you want to stick with, you may wish to purchase your domain name and your hosting plan for a few years out.

This will allow you to rest easy knowing that you won't have to worry about your domain name expiring (and possibly getting snatched up by someone else) and your site going offline because you forgot to renew.

Once you've got your domain name purchased and hosting plan locked in, the next step is to install the WordPress platform. In fact, this is a great way to test the technical support staff of your new hosting company by calling them up and asking them to guide you through the WordPress setup.

A Word about WordPress

Without getting too technical, the web is built using computer code called HTML (HyperText Markup Language). For a long time, only tech geeks who knew how to write and manipulate code had the power to build sites on the web. However, with the creation of CMS (Content Management System) platforms like WordPress (Joomla and Drupal are two other names in CMS), the playing field opened up to allow just about anyone to learn how to build and maintain a website, regardless of their technical knowledge.

These open-source CMS platforms offer an easy graphic user interface (GUI—referred to as "gooey" by techies) that allows you to build a site even if you don't know how to code. These CMS sites are still using HTML code, but it's running behind the scenes and you don't have to worry about it unless you want to. As you get more advanced, you can go into the source code and manipulate it to change the look or functionality of your WordPress site if you want.

You can customize your WordPress website by using "Themes," which will dictate how your site looks to the viewer. There are both free and premium themes available all over the web that can make your site look amazing. I like to use the analogy of a car: your Theme is the body of the car, or how it looks on the outside. WordPress is the engine running the theme, and HTML code is the gas that's running the engine.

If you decide to build a site using WordPress, you have two options: you can either get free hosting on wordpress.COM and build your site there (in which case your domain would be "yourname.wordpress.com"), or you can purchase your own hosting plan from any hosting company, load the free WordPress software available from wordpress.ORG (the WordPress software is also available in the back-end control panel of your hosting account), and run your own self-hosted site using whatever domain name you choose (e.g., "MyAwesomeArt.com").

I recommend the second option because I feel it's important to have your own space on the web, but you can investigate your options and go with the one that feels right to you. (See Resources for links to WordPress themes, hosting companies and domain registrars).

Now that you've got your domain, hosting and WordPress in place, it's time to populate your site with content.

WordPress Plug-Ins

NERD ALERT: This section gets pretty technical (i.e., dry). If you're somewhat familiar with the dashboard of WordPress, dive in. If you're not there yet, feel free to skip ahead for now.

On the wordpress.org site, there is link to a page dedicated to plug-ins. These are add-on applications that work within WordPress to do specific things that aren't already included in the platform. When you click the plug-ins page mentioned above, you will see page after page of free apps that developers have created to make your website experience easier, better, more convenient, etc. There are way more available than you actually need, but there are a few that are essential and will make your life easier.

Akismet – This is a spam detector that prevents people from posting spammy comments to your site. One of the cool things about WordPress is that it allows viewers to comment on your posts and pages, which provides an interactive channel of communication between you and your audience. Unfortunately, shady characters and dubious marketers have discovered this as a new channel to target with their spam. I get hundreds of spam comments per week on my website, but thankfully, Akismet catches almost all of them, and places them in a spam folder that I just have to empty when I log in.

You can download Akismet from the WordPress plug-ins page, then upload it to your site. When you activate this, you will prompted to visit Akismet's website to get an API key, which is needed to run the app. This plug-in used to be free, but now when you go to get your API key, they ask how much this plug-in is worth to you, and you can use a slider to indicate a monthly "donation" amount. I always feel guilty if I leave the slider at "0" because it's a great little app, but you can make your own decision.

All In One SEO Pack – This is another must-have plug-in if you want to increase your website's chances of getting found via search. I've also been happy with **WordPress SEO by Yoast**, but it requires slightly more advanced knowledge of the strategic use of search terms.

SEO stands for Search Engine Optimization, and basically is a way of ensuring that your site gets found on the web by search engines like Google, Yahoo! and Bing. SEO is an ever-changing game, so it's very difficult to try to keep up with the latest ways to rank high on search results. Using All In One SEO is an easy way to include important search data on each page and post on your website, which will increase your chances of ranking well with search engines.

All In One SEO uses keywords to help the search engines properly categorize your site. Once you install the plug-in, there will be an area at the bottom of each page and post (on the back-end of the site) containing text fields where you will enter your Title, Description and relevant Keywords. Let's say you're creating your Statement page. When it comes to naming the page that appears in the navigation menu on your site, you are writing for humans to read, so you can simply name the page "Artist Statement."

However, for SEO purposes, you are writing for search engine spiders that crawl your site and try to glean info that helps them categorize your content. Therefore, in the All In One SEO text field labeled 'Title', you want to include additional information indicating Who, What and Where. That may be something like, "Artist Statement for Watercolor Painter Jane Smith Brooklyn NY."

Then in the 'Description' field, you can expound on that and add more descriptive phrases, including your Three Adjectives you have decided upon. Your character count is somewhat limited, so keep your description concise and try to include the most relevant descriptive words (making sure you're including your Who, What and Where), and try to leave out little, non-essential words like 'a', 'the', 'at', 'in', 'and', etc.

In the 'Keywords' section, you want to enter as many relevant keywords and phrases you can think of and separate them with a comma. With so many artists in the world, your chances of ranking well for generic words like 'art', 'artist', 'painters', 'watercolor artist', etc. are pretty slim. Therefore you want to focus your efforts on more specific phrases: "brooklyn artists, artists in Brooklyn, watercolor artists in new york, jane smith brooklyn artist," etc.

Capitalization isn't important to search engines, but commas are. Putting commas after each word is telling the search engine to look for those specific words, and placing them after a string of words is telling them to look for that specific phrase.

The idea here is to think about how people look for things on the web. Let's say a gallery owner in Brooklyn, NY, wanted to reach out to local artists for an exhibit. The first thing she would type into Google would be "artists in brooklyn ny" or "brooklyn artists." If your site contains those keywords, it will appear somewhere in the search results.

By knowing what types of phrases people are using to find work like yours, you will have a good idea of the kinds of keywords and phrases you should use on your own site.

Mailing List Sign-Up – Another imperative item to include on your website is a mailing list sign-up box. This is where visitors to your website can enter their names and email addresses and join your email list electronically. You want to have a sign-up box visible on your home page, and on every page within your site.

You can do this easily by putting it into a widget area in the sidebar of your WordPress site. Of course, this is only necessary if you plan on sending out regular communications to your audience, which you should.

The email marketing service you decide to use will usually have tools such as a sign-up box for your website to help you grow your list. Some of them are more customizable than others and some are pretty standard. Once you choose or customize the look of your sign-up box, you are given a snippet of HTML code that you place into areas of your site such as pages, posts and widget areas.

There are WordPress plug-ins that allow you to create sign-up boxes as well, which you can find by going to WordPress.org and searching the Plug-Ins page for "mailing list sign-up" or "newsletter sign-up." There are also third-party applications that are available for purchase, such as Pippity and Pop-Up Domination (see Resources) that allow you to create good-looking sign-up boxes and pop-ups that will help you grow your list.

There are many more plug-ins available that may be helpful to use on your WordPress site, but these are three that I recommend using right off the bat. As you get more familiar with the platform you will discover more plug-ins and other tools to benefit your website that you may wish to implement. One word of caution: it's easy to go overboard. If your site is so bogged down with gewgaws and gadgets that its performance or load time suffers, then it is time to edit selectively.

Website Page Order

All the information you compile for your Artist Packet can be used on the pages of your website as well. The only additional thing you'll need to create is the About Page and a Contact Page, both of which we discuss below. Here is a list of items included on a typical artist website:

1) About Page – See below
2) Artist Statement – Use info from Artist Packet
3) Artist Bio – Use info from Artist Packet
4) Contact Page – See below
5) Portfolio – Big, beautiful pictures of your art
6) Blog – Optional. See To Blog or Not to Blog? below

About the Artist – The About Page should tell readers a little bit about who you are as a person and an artist. This differs from your Artist Statement in that your About Page is about YOU as a person, and your Statement is specifically about the ART you are presenting. Your About Page doesn't have to be a dry, chronological recounting of your life, but it should give some insight into your personality, your life experience, and what led you to where you are now. Feel free to let your own voice shine through in your writing. Tell your story and have fun with it.

Make your About Page unique and memorable, and don't stress out thinking it has to follow certain "rules." Write it as a haiku, a recipe, a story or a fairy tale—just make sure that it represents your unique creative voice and gives readers a little understanding of who you are. If you get stuck and need inspiration, visit the websites of other artists to see how they represent themselves, but make sure your end result is original and distinctive.

And, for the love of Pete, include a photo of yourself! There are so many sites out there, personal and business alike, that don't include the proprietor's own photo on their About Page. This comes off as impersonal and faceless—no matter how good the rest of the site is. In fact, when business sites try to present themselves as all Mom-and-Pop-y, yet don't include a photo of the owners or the founders on the About Page, they come off as suspect, and you begin to wonder if they're legit. You are legit and you are creative. Take a creative photo and post it on this page!

Artist Statement and Bio – You've already spent time writing these for your Artist Packet, so simply cut and paste each document into a page of its own and label it accordingly. In order to add a little visual interest to these pages, you can also include photos that aren't already included on your Portfolio Page (no sense showing duplicates). They can either be additional images of your art, or they can be fun, candid photos of you at exhibits and art openings or in your studio.

Contact Page – This page should include all the different ways to contact you. You may not want to include your home address, but you can list your email address, phone number and links to your social media profiles. If you're concerned about privacy or spam, this page could simply contain a contact form, where people fill out their name, email address and inquiry or comment and hit a "Submit" button that sends you an email without listing any of your personal information. Personally, I like to make it as easy as possible for interested parties to contact me, but it's important that you do what's comfortable for you.

Portfolio – The main reason for having a website is to display your art, so the portfolio aspect is essential. Remember the WordPress themes mentioned above? When searching for themes, look for ones that are photo-centric. In fact there is a whole category of portfolio themes that have been specifically created for artists and photographers who wish to display their work prominently on their site.

Whatever theme you choose, you want to make sure your images are big, easy to access and user-friendly to scroll through. I've purchased several themes that I ended up abandoning later because I found the image navigation wasn't as user-friendly as I had hoped.

When you're shopping for WordPress themes, they often have live previews that you can poke around on to get an idea of the functionality. Unfortunately, you never really know how effective the theme is going to be for your purposes until you buy it, install it and set it up according to the documentation that accompanies it. As for documentation, some of the developers creating WordPress themes include excellent step-by-step instructions for setting up and customizing your theme, and others have vague, incomplete instructions written in broken English that are quite frustrating.

Before I buy a new theme, I always check out the support forum and see what people are complaining about and how responsive the developer has been to the people commenting.

When it comes to displaying your images online, make sure the WordPress themes you're considering are geared towards showcasing art. It takes time to wade through the thousands of themes available, test the demos and investigate the support forums, but if it helps you choose a great theme that represents your style of work, the extra effort is worthwhile.

The Online Portfolio Option

An alternative to building your own website is to set up a presence on one (or more) of the many portfolio sites available. These are existing websites that cater to artists who want their work to be visible online, but don't want to take the effort or time to deal with the technical and maintenance commitment of running their own website.

That is probably one of the biggest attractions of choosing an online portfolio site: you don't have to concern yourself with the technical side of running a website. All you have to do is set up an account, fill in your profile information, upload photos of your art, and you're off to the races. In order to maximize your visibility on the web, you can even set up an account with several online portfolio sites. Depending on the site, you will still need to be an active member of the online community and do some occasional updates and maintenance, so don't think you can just "set it and forget it" on a whole bunch of sites and call it a day.

Another benefit of having your work on an artist portfolio site is that the organization running the site, and the other artists featured on the site, are presumably doing their part to promote it. That means the site should already have a decent flow of traffic, which increases the possibility of visitors stumbling upon your work.

However, the larger the community of artists on the site, the more likely your work becomes the proverbial needle in the haystack. Therefore, you cannot simply sit back and hope your art is discovered by the residual traffic. You are still fully responsible for driving traffic to your portfolio, which will have its own custom URL.

One of the drawbacks of taking this route is that you are not building equity in your creative brand as much as you're building equity in the site that you are aligning with. It's kind of like the difference between renting an apartment in a high-rise complex with tons of other tenants—which benefits your landlord— versus owning your own home in the city, which builds equity for you. Whether you are talking about renting versus owning in the real world or the virtual world, there are pros and cons related to each scenario. The question then becomes, which one is right for you?

Whether you choose to join an online community site or launch and maintain your own website, you should still view your online presence as supplemental to your real-life exhibits. And each should drive reciprocal traffic to the other, meaning that you use your online tools to promote your real-world exhibits, and at your openings you promote your online presence.

I've listed a few portfolio sites in the Resources section for you to visit: you can investigate them and see if this is an appropriate route to take for your online presence.

To Blog or Not to Blog?

Deciding to maintain a blog is a decision that should not be taken lightly, because it is a long-term commitment. Too many people have decided they would create a blog in a moment of inspired passion, only to lose steam and fizzle out after a couple of months. You don't need to add to the abundance of abandoned blogs floating in the cybersphere, so be certain that you've got something valuable—and sustainable—to offer before you begin blogging.

A Very Brief History of Blogging

There is some confusion surrounding blogs, so I'll spend a moment to clarify what they are and how they are different from typical websites. Way back in the late '90s, just before the dawn of the new millennium, there were a handful of sites on the web that contained links, commentary, personal thoughts and insights around various subjects.

While this is very commonplace today, it was very novel at the time. These sites were dubbed "weblogs" as they contained a "log" of links and ideas on the "web," and a small community sprang up around this activity.

By 2000, the trend caught fire. The term "weblogs" had been truncated to "blogs," weblog editors were now "bloggers" and online tools became available to make blogging easier and more accessible to the common folk. This was a huge paradigm shift that allowed ordinary people access to a world-wide medium, which was typically the realm of huge corporations and communist governments. Throughout the aughts, blogs morphed from personal online journals to robust vehicles for engaging in substantial communication with a (potentially) world-wide audience.

> "*Your blog is a media property. It's also a tool that allows you to build relationships, to notify and inform, to reflect and react, report, or a tool to educate, instruct, or establish thought leadership. It can be a call to action, a lead generator, a showcase for your talents, and many other things. The question is: what will you choose as your focus, and how do you define its purpose?*"

– Chris Brogan, Social Media Blogger and Author

The difference between a website and a blog is this: websites contain static content and information that people can access as needed, similar to an online brochure. Static websites are helpful and informative for first-time visitors, but once they've visited, there's no incentive for them to return.

Adding a blog to your website lets you create fresh, dynamic content that draws visitors back to your site over and over again. This is a good thing, since increasing website traffic is the primary goal of anyone with an online property. Another benefit to WordPress is that it allows you to easily build either a static website—if you don't plan on blogging—or a dynamic website that contains a blog—if you do plan to maintain a blog.

Benefits of Blogging

There are many benefits of blogging, and if you decide to maintain a blog, you should know why you are doing so. The days of blogs simply acting as personal journals are long gone. Instead, you want to create quality content that provides some sort of value to your readers and post it at regular intervals. This will improve traffic to your site by giving people a reason to return, and will also benefit you in the following ways:

Improving SEO – When people are looking for something on the web, search engines want to provide the most relevant and up-to-date info. They frequently send out crawlers, spiders and bots to every corner of the web looking for active sites with fresh data and high levels of traffic, links and engagement.

Once they crawl the web, search engines categorize everything they find so they can serve up the info when needed. When the bots visit a static website that hasn't changed in months, they put it low on their list of relevance. Conversely, when they find a dynamic site with fresh content, they see it as an active hub and will give it a better rank in its category, which will help get you found.

The way SEO works is actually quite complicated and always changing, but maintaining a consistent blog is a sure-fire way to get search engines to notice your site.

Creating a Dynamic Web Presence – The SEO benefit mentioned above will help you get found online by people who are searching for generic or random art terms. However, you also want to show a dynamic web presence for people who meet you, hear about you or discover your name and do a follow-up search looking to learn more about you.

Since an active blog contains several posts that are categorized separately by search engines, a search for your name will bring up an ever-growing list of results. This isn't merely a vanity metric; it shows that you are active in the digital space and adds to your "social proof." This gives you further legitimacy and allows you to extend your reach to friends, family, fans and art collectors around the world.

Building a Following – Sure, you could simply build a website that features your art and leave it at that. However, maintaining an active blog has far-reaching effects that can help you get noticed and build relationships with the audience that you are trying to reach. Marketing should be similar to holding an ongoing conversation. By sharing artwork, opinions and ideas on your blog and allowing your audience to chime in via the Comments section, you are able to hold a dialogue with a potential world-wide audience.

Capturing Contact Info – As I've mentioned, you want to feature a mailing list opt-in box on your site to capture email addresses of your visitors. However, if you simply have a static site that doesn't change much, the visitors won't be very inclined to join your mailing list.

On the other hand, if you're frequently updating your blog with fresh, exciting content and utilizing various marketing tools and tactics to direct traffic to your blog, there will be a steady stream of regular and new visitors coming to your site to engage with your content. Creating an active community around your blog will increase the number of people who join your mailing list, especially if you offer some sort of incentive to do so (we'll talk more about incentives shortly).

There are other benefits, but I won't belabor the point here. If you think you're interested in blogging, there are tons of sites on the web that are geared towards helping people create successful blogs. There are also sites by artists and arts organizations that maintain blogs that are worth investigating. The information that's out there may be helpful to you both as an artist and as a potential blogger.

Blogging is a lot of work and it's certainly not for everybody, but if done right, it can be a powerful, effective, stimulating way to create a vital online presence that will get you noticed by the very people you are trying to reach with your art. One of the best bits of advice I can give about blogging—and marketing in general—is to "make it about them."

Sorry to say, but no matter how much someone loves your art, if all your communication outreach is about you, you, you, people will lose interest rather quickly. Why? Because no matter how fascinating you are, people find themselves to be even more fascinating! Therefore, you must find a way to make your blog content relevant to the lives, needs, curiosities and desires of your audience.

> *"Using blogging software is not a trend or tool or even a behavior, it's the single most important marketing element of your Total Online Presence. It puzzles me why people still fight this notion or why they would ever consider entrusting their content assets to Facebook or some other social network flavor of the month."*
>
> – John Jantsch, DuctTape Marketing

Creating a Successful Blog

The most common mistake people make when blogging is to peter out after an initial burst of activity. It's fun and exciting to start a blog; the hard part is maintaining it over time. There are millions of blogs out in cyberspace, and a large percentage of them are inactive, outdated wastelands offering testament to their former author's short-lived passion. Try not to make the same mistake!

When attempting to create a relevant, ongoing, successful web property that your audience will enjoy visiting, carefully consider the following elements:

Post Frequency – How often should you post? This will depend on several factors, such as the feasibility of your writing schedule, how much you have to say on a particular topic, as well as the desires, schedules and lifestyles of your readers. Post too frequently and it's overwhelming and hard to keep up; post too infrequently and your audience forgets about you or loses interest; post just the right amount and you can build an engaged audience that looks forward to reading your consistently enjoyable content.

I was following a marketing blog where the author posted seven days a week! I had to unsubscribe because I was getting so far behind in my reading. There are pro bloggers who advise posting 3–5 times a week, but I feel that's a very difficult pace to maintain. Personally, I aim to post twice a month on my art marketing blog (DeathToTheStarvingArtist.com), but even that can be a challenge.

Not only because I have a busy schedule, but also because I write long, detailed posts that are packed with tips and info, which take time to come up with. At the very minimum, I would recommend posting 2–3 times per month. This is probably too infrequent for your audience to depend on; therefore, when you do post new content, you must employ your other marketing tools, such as social media, email newsletters, etc., to drive traffic to your new posts.

Blog Content – Once you decide you are going to maintain a blog, the first question that usually pops up is, "What am I going to write about?" The following topics will give you content ideas that you can expand on and embellish. Just remember that you are attempting to create or encourage a dialogue between you and your audience, rather than just blast out post after post of "me, me, me" information.

- **Behind the Scenes** – People love to get a glimpse of the workings that go on behind the curtain. It makes them feel like they are gaining access to something slightly exclusive. Post photos and videos of you in various places and scenarios such as your studio workspace, at the gallery prepping for an exhibit, or "backstage" at any other promotional or creative event. You can even post about your visits to galleries, museums or events by other artists, whether they are friends of yours or famous names that you appreciate and admire.

This allows your audience to glean insights about your life, your activities and your personal tastes. People want to know that there is more to an artist than the finished work they pump out or the calculated façade they present to the public, so give your audience a little peek at what makes you tick as a person as well as an artist.

I'm crazy about Andy Warhol, so visiting his "Warhol: Live" exhibition in 2009 at the De Young Museum in San Francisco was a treat. Photography was not allowed in the exhibit, but there was no way I was going to give up the chance to document this once-in-a-lifetime experience. So, I snuck my camera in and took stealth shots in every room of the exhibit. Later, I created a blog post about my experience—complete with forbidden photos—as well as a Facebook photo album, both of which generated much engagement.

• **In-Progress Photos** – I've seen time-lapse videos of artists producing their creations and it's always fascinating to see the process and progress as a piece moves towards its finished state. It's also fun to see still images of the various stages a piece of art goes through on its way to completion. Keep a digital camera in your studio and capture your progress so you can post about the evolution of your art. One thing I will mention here is that it pays to know how to edit yourself. When telling a visual story, shoot plenty of photos, but be selective with the ones you choose to tell the final story. I see people using their blog—and more often, Facebook—as a veritable photo dump, where they upload every photo they took at the party, or the opening, or their camping vacation. That's a lazy approach that diminishes both the quality and interest of the viewer experience. Take the time to be selective and tell a concise, progressive visual story with your photos.

- **How-To Tips** – The entirety of your audience is not going to be made up of buyers and collectors. Your blog will also attract your peers and other artists. One way to keep their attention and make it relevant to them is to share your knowledge of art-related subjects that you are proficient in.

This could include things such as canvas-wrapping, framing, lighting or photographing artwork, or even special painting or drawing techniques. In fact, I started posting marketing tips on one of my early art websites, which was the launching point for me to create a separate website focusing entirely on marketing, which became my company blog for BAM! Small Biz Consulting. Don't hoard your knowledge: share it with your audience while you simultaneously build your own reputation as a skilled expert.

One thing worth mentioning is that I don't think you should give everything away for free forever. If you find your audience growing and the demand for your skills expanding, don't be afraid to capitalize on this by moving to a paid model. This could be accomplished by turning your content into an educational product for sale such as ebooks, a video series or webinars, or even creating a subscription-based website.

- **Videos** – I've mentioned videos several times throughout this book. The success of YouTube shows just how much people enjoy a rich-media experience. Many people approach video with the attempt to "make it go viral." The challenge is that we never really know what's going to go viral until it happens, so trying to reverse-engineer a viral video is pointless. Instead, you should simply focus on making your video compelling, honest and real. Or, depending on your own point-of-view and personality, you can take a silly, fun and engaging route as well.

However, the biggest tip is this: keep it short! Generally, the maximum length of most of your videos should be no longer than three and a half minutes (3:30). There are exceptions that I will mention when we discuss YouTube as a marketing tool, but for now keep the three-minute mark as your target. The reason is simply because people have short attention spans, and it's better to leave them wanting more than to have them tune out and click off your page. As for video content, consider the three previous bullet points (Behind the Scenes, Works in Progress, and How-To Tips) as starting points. Once you get used to using video as an expressive medium, you can expand from there, but start by turning the camera on your own creative process to create a deeper connection with your audience.

As you can see, creating and maintaining a blog not only takes focus, effort and commitment, but also turns you into a media producer. Once you make the decision to become a blogger, there's no turning back if you want to create anything that matters, or resonates with your audience. In fact, there's something that I call "living with a blog mentality," which means you are always thinking about how each meaningful moment, event or creative session can be an opportunity to capture and create content to post on your blog.

This very idea may seem repugnant to many people, and I'll admit, it's a responsibility that can take you "out of the moment" occasionally. However, in our media-saturated culture, it will give you a leg up on the competition to utilize all the amazing tools at your disposal in order to reach a world-wide market. Using your blog as an opportunity to share, educate, entertain and provide value to your audience will allow you to create a powerful media property and a successful marketing tool that can connect you to the people who will make a difference in your creative career.

3.4

Growing Your Mailing List

I've mentioned your mailing list a few times already, so let's talk about how to set it up and use it for maximum marketing effectiveness. The reason a mailing list is so important is because it gives an opportunity for people who are interested in you and your work to "opt in" to your communications. Essentially, they are giving you permission to communicate with them. I should mention here that you never want to add people to your mailing list without their permission. When it comes to your list, quality is better than quantity; besides, you don't want to ruin your reputation by becoming known as a spammer.

In order for your communication to be effective you need to find a delicate balance between keeping in touch with your audience, marketing to them and providing them with some kind of value that is relevant to their lives. People will join your mailing list for various reasons: they know you; they respond to your work; they are curious to hear more from you; or you provide them with an attractive incentive to join. Some may even sign out of guilt because they didn't have the courage to say no when you asked them to join.

Usually, everyone who joins is doing so on a trial basis. They want to see what kind of communication they are going to receive and how it's going to benefit THEM. If your email newsletters skew too promotional, your audience will start unsubscribing. Likewise, if your communication is boring, non-relevant to your audience, or too focused on YOU, they will start dropping like flies. This may seem paradoxical because, after all, they did sign YOUR mailing list. But it bears repeating that the reason people do anything is because they think somehow—even in the most minute way—that it is going to make their lives better, easier or more enjoyable.

Therefore, you should aim to make your newsletters something that your audience will look forward to receiving and reading. We'll discuss content ideas in a moment, but for now let's figure out how to get people signed up!

Working Your List at Events

You can create your own sign-up sheet in your favorite computer program like Word, Excel or Adobe Illustrator, or you can purchase a date book or notebook for people to sign. Whichever route you choose, make sure your name and contact information is clearly visible on every page, so there is no mistake about whose list it is. Your sign-up sheet should have visible rows that will keep things easy and orderly, and there should be several columns for the information you wish to collect.

Most of the time, people are willing to supply their name and email, so there should be a minimum of two columns. It's also nice to have a home mailing address so you can send the occasional postcard, but people are usually hesitant to give that information out. If you don't ask for their home address on your mailing list, make sure you have a procedure in place to procure the home address of anyone who buys something from you. People who sign your mailing list are expressing a slight interest and curiosity about your work, so email communication is sufficient.

People who actually purchase your work are making a deeper commitment, and you can communicate with them at a deeper level of engagement, such as sending postcards, thank-you cards, follow-up notes and holiday greetings to their home. So, whether it's a receipt booklet, a credit card information form, or even your own information-gathering database, get full contact info from your actual customers at the buying stage.

One thing you want to avoid is people thinking your mailing list is simply a guest list. I see this happening at some of my clients' businesses. I worked with a restaurant that had amassed a dozen binders filled with signatures, comments and complaints from guests throughout the years. While all these books may be fun keepsakes for nostalgic memorabilia, they are worthless as marketing tools because none of the guests were leaving their contact information! If the restaurant wanted to appease an unsatisfied customer or reach out to a frequent guest, they had no way to get in touch with these people.

I saw the same thing happening when I was working at Liberty Arts Gallery. While a lot of the visitors left their name and email address in the guest book, many of them simply wrote their names and where they were from. The key here is to make clearly labeled columns so the guests know what information you want from them, and conversely, you need to convey what it is they will be receiving from you as well.

You must give people a reason to sign up, so let them know what they will be receiving and how often. Whether you display a table tent or label near your sign-up book, have a brief sentence written on each page of the book, or choose to tell people verbally when you ask them to join, you must let people know what's in it for them. One example that you often see is, "Please join my mailing list to receive monthly newsletters about art and upcoming events."

Obviously, you can create your own incentives, offers and frequency and even inject a little of your own personality into it. Whatever you do, avoid simply posing the question, "Do you want to join my mailing list?" Instead, give your audience a compelling reason to WANT to join your list.

One of the downsides of exhibiting your work outside of your area is that you are not always able to be present at the opening of the show. You could send a mailing list along with the art and ask the gallery staff to display it near your work on opening night, but that's leaving an awful lot to chance. The best approach is to attend as many openings as possible. A close second is to make sure you're integrating your other marketing tools in a way that "completes the circle."

For example, your website is up and running and you have a mailing list sign-up box—with a compelling call to action—in a visible location on it. An exhibition of your work opens in a city that you cannot attend, but you have your artist statement, bio and/or postcards on display at the opening and they all list your website URL. Any interested parties can visit your website, see your call to action and join your mailing list if they so desire. Some of the email marketing programs, such as Constant Contact, also have a text-to-join option. If you incorporate that, you can print your mailing-list call to action right on the aforementioned print collateral and allow people to join your list by texting a specified number with their smartphones.

Collecting Business Cards

One great tactic for growing your list is to hold prize drawings at each of your events. Have some sort of container that people can drop their business cards in for a chance to win an 8" × 10" print of your art, or a five-minute portrait sketch, or a six-pack of your art cards. The idea is to make the prize compelling enough to make people want to give up their info for it, but not so grand that you end up going broke from giving away the farm.

The key is to have a small sign near your collection box that details WHAT you're giving away (your prize), HOW they can enter to win (dropping their biz card in the box), and HOW they will be notified (by email). Since email marketing is an opt-in practice, you should also include the fine print that "By entering this drawing, you agree to receive email communication from the artist."

3.5

Email Marketing Platforms

There are several email marketing platforms in the game (see Resources), but when it comes down to it, there are two names that you hear the most: Mail Chimp and Constant Contact. As far as competitors go, these two platforms both offer robust solutions that are easy and fun to use, and each can produce quality, professional communications that make you look good.

The big difference is that Mail Chimp is free, while Constant Contact starts around $25 per month and goes up from there depending on the features you use. Don't let that be your only deciding factor, however, as "free" doesn't always mean better. I use and appreciate both platforms, and while I use Mail Chimp for some of my clients' communications, I prefer Constant Contact for my own email marketing.

Here's a breakdown of the two platforms:

Mail Chimp
- **Cost** – Did I mention it was free? This makes MC a no-brainer for many people.

- **Great Analytics** – MC makes it fun to view reports of who received your email, who opened it, and who clicked on your links. The charts and graphs are easy to read and offer great insight into what you're doing right and wrong in the eyes of your audience. There have been several times that someone told me they didn't receive an email. After a quick check of the analytics, I was able to reply, "Yes, you did, actually. You opened it on December 7th at 9:32am."

- **Social Media Integration** – When Mail Chimp came out, they were immediately superior in the area of social media integration, but over time Constant Contact has made great strides in this department. Email marketing needs to be integrated into all the other marketing tools you're using, and MC makes it easy to share and connect your newsletters to your social media accounts.

- **User Interface Could Be Better** – The MC brand is funny and cheeky and that is obvious throughout their design. The overall interface is good—and they keep tweaking it for improvement—but the main text editor is one long, scrolling window containing ALL the text, photos and links in the document you're working on, which is a little bit precarious and not as user-friendly as CC's module editor.

In fact, more than once, I have spent time crafting my perfect newsletter copy for several articles, only to somehow have it all disappear, or not get saved, or kick me out of the editor window when I hit the Delete button to fix a typo.

- **Limited Template Designs** – In the free account, the template designs you have access to are pretty limited, and quite frankly, they all look pretty similar. However, they are pretty customizable, so I have been able to make some attractive newsletters and announcements, and have seen other people do so as well. Mail Chimp also offers paid, or premium accounts, which give you access to lots of custom designs by an increasing community of artists and designers.

- **Attractive Sign-Up Box** – Mail Chimp allows you to create a custom sign-up box to post on your other web properties, through which people can join your list. It allows you to easily generate a snippet of HTML code that creates a sign-up box allowing your viewers to enter their name, email and other information right in the box where they find it, rather than take you offsite to a separate page to enter your info. This is super important for easily capturing leads at the moment your web visitors express interest, without driving them off your site.

- **Can't Send to Multiple Lists** – The inability to select multiple lists when sending your newsletter is Mail Chimp's biggest mistake. Instead, for each list you have, they make you duplicate, triplicate and quadruplicate your email and send each version to a separate list. This results in tremendous amounts of confusion and wasted time, and is utterly inefficient! MC claims that people who are on more than one list (which is quite common) WILL NOT get more than one email, but I have received several complaints from people who were getting two or three copies of the same email. In order to alleviate the frustration of my audience, I ended up having to consolidate my four lists into one big list. This means every email that goes out is received by the entire list, which is not always appropriate. Epic fail.

If you're just getting started with email marketing, Mail Chimp is a solid choice. When you're facing a learning curve, it's nice to keep your investment low so you can familiarize yourself with the platform at your own pace. In time, you may find that Mail Chimp is the right platform for you and stick with it. Or not. I started off using Constant Contact, then switched to Mail Chimp when I was trying to trim my budget. I quickly learned that some things are worth the investment, so I switched back to CC.

While I enjoy Mail Chimp, I have found I prefer Constant Contact for my own use. But, as I mentioned, I still use them both. The truth is, there are frustrating aspects with both platforms, but in my mind, the $25 per month I spend on Constant Contact is money well spent.

Let's examine some of the pros and cons of this platform:

Constant Contact
- **60-Day Trial** – Constant Contact offers a two-month free trial, which is plenty of time to learn how to use the platform and determine if it's right for you.

- **Monthly Fee** – A basic account starts at $15 per month if you have less than 500 contacts. There are a couple of necessary add-ons for extra photo storage capacity and the ability to archive your emails that each cost $5 extra per month, so to get started, you're looking at about $20–30 per month. The monthly cost goes up as your list grows, and there are other available options that add to the price as well.

- **Very Good User Interface** – Constant Contact has a user interface that is a bit more robust than Mail Chimp's, but it is pretty intuitive and easy to pick up. CC leads you through the process of creating, testing and sending email communications in a way that's easy to get the hang of. One great feature is that the email templates contain individual modules that can each be edited separately. Plus, they can be dragged and moved easily if you want to rearrange the layout of your template.

  Over the years, CC has continued to make improvements to the user experience, which shows a commitment to continued excellence that is necessary for a company that wants to maintain relevance.

- **Good Selection of Designs** – There is a wide selection of email templates to choose from and they are filtered by categories, which makes it easy to browse appropriate looks for each industry. The templates are customizable, so you can find designs that appeal to you and proceed to make them your own.

- **Good Analytics** – It's important to understand what's working and what isn't working with your email communications, and CC makes it easy with their analytic reports. Mail Chimp puts more focus on analytics, featuring report graphs and subscriber activity from your latest email on the first page when you log in. The analytic results are buried a bit deeper in Constant Contact, but they do exist and are great for measuring the results of your communications.

- **Social Media Integration** – Constant Contact was playing catch-up with Mail Chimp for a long time in the area of social media. Then they decided to get serious and have even acquired other social startup companies in order to improve their offerings. Now it's super easy to include social share buttons right in the header of your email and place links to your own social networks in the body of the email.

  Another great feature allows you to post your emails to your various social networks at the same time you dispatch them to your list. You can even customize the title and description for each network. When your fans and followers click the link from your social profiles, your newsletter opens as a page in their web browser.

- **Outdated Opt-In Boxes** – My biggest pet peeve with Constant Contact is their opt-in boxes, which seem like they haven't evolved since the '90s. You would think a company that revolves around opt-in marketing would totally rock their opt-in boxes. Not! Epic fail.

Compelling Email Content is Key

So, what kind of content are you sending out through these various email platforms? First, let's be clear on one thing: using plain text emails for your art marketing won't cut it anymore. Communicating via email through your Yahoo! and Gmail accounts is fine for family and friends, and for informational business exchanges, but not for representing your art. A rich visual medium such as fine art deserves to be represented in a way that showcases it—and you—in the best way possible.

Email Newsletters

I've been using this term as the example throughout this section, so let's start there. Sending out a monthly newsletter to your list is a great way to stay top-of-mind with your audience. As for the content of the newsletter, you can include updates as to what's happening in your career, offer sneak previews of new works, announce upcoming shows, show which of your pieces have sold recently, and share feedback, quotes or testimonials.

One of my clients runs a gallery, and I produce their monthly newsletter. My favorite section is called "Overheard," where I include three short quotes or phrases uttered by gallery visitors as they peruse the exhibitions. Some are positive, some are critical, but they always offer a fun, fly-on-the-wall perspective of how people respond to art.

Including fun or personal bits of content in your newsletters will give your readers something enjoyable to look forward to in addition to all your serious, "just the facts, ma'am" art news.

Your mailing list will surely include your peers and other artists who are also seeking value, so perhaps your newsletter could include educational tips that relate to your medium of choice. This could include topics such as painting techniques, brush-cleaning, buying supplies, framing, packing and shipping artworks, or product recommendations.

Hopefully, your list will also contain collectors and buyers who would appreciate insight into the industry. For example, there was a fascinating and scandalous story that emerged in 2012 about a New York gallery selling counterfeit works from big-name artists. If you include links to stories like that in your newsletter, you could then summarize the story in your own words and include tips on things to watch out for when buying art.

You can also include news blurbs, stories or links to other interesting happenings in the art world. For example, when Sotheby's sold Edvard Munch's *Scream* for nearly $120 million, your newsletter might have included a sidebar blurb with your thoughts or comments, a related photo and a link to one of the many in-depth articles on the web. Or if an artist you like is included in a museum exhibit, or is in the news for an anniversary event or milestone, you can include a mention in your newsletter.

In other words, you don't have to make everything about YOU, but can also put the focus on the world of art, the business of art, or the artists that you admire or count as influences. Doing so will make your newsletters well-rounded, enjoyable pieces of communication that your audience looks forward to receiving.

Taking all of the above into consideration may seem like your newsletter is a never-ending scroll-fest featuring hours of reading material. Not quite. The key is to keep each newsletter brief, so it is informative but still leaves your audience wanting more. If you include blocks and blocks of text, your audience will tune out quickly. Keep your descriptions short and your photos enticing, and use your newsletter as a bridge to carry people back to your website.

If people are interested in the teaser articles in the newsletter, they can click through to your blog, which should contain the longer versions of the articles, tips and events featured in your newsletter. As for additional newsletter articles that you did not write, such as those detailing the Munch sale and the gallery scandal mentioned above, your teaser articles can link to other websites and articles on the web as well.

If you decide you are not going to be blogging, your newsletter can simply contain brief articles relating to your chosen content. Instead of linking back to your site for the full article, just make sure each short article contains all the details your reader needs. If you take this route, you should still look for a reason to include at least one or two links back to your website—your portfolio page in particular—because your mantra should always be "drive traffic to my site!"

Every edition of your newsletter should also include your full contact information and links to your social media profiles. Hopefully, you will start to see how every marketing tool you are using is interconnected, which compounds and amplifies your efforts to reach a larger audience.

Email Invitations

When you have an exhibit approaching, it's imperative to utilize all the tools in your arsenal to spread the word. Of course, a beautiful email invitation is at the top of the list (other essentials are postcards, Facebook Events, and press releases).

Your email invitations should include the following:

- Enticing Subject line that will get your email opened (e.g., "You Are Invited an Enchanting Evening of Art" or "Experience Smashing Sensory Stimuli This Friday Night!")

- Concise Headline that clarifies the Subject line

- A great Photo that links back to your website portfolio or event post containing more details

- Short, descriptive Body Copy that explains how awesome your event will be and why the reader shouldn't even think of missing it. Remember to make this about THEM. Try to craft the copy in a way that describes the fun THEY will have, rather than just being about YOUR involvement.

- What, When, Where summary in bullet point form (for the scanners who don't like to read full sentences)

- Your Name and Contact Info so people can reach you with questions or directions

- Website Link and Call to Action (e.g., "Visit my website for all the deets"), especially if you have more details or directions on your site

Email Announcements

These are similar to Invitations and should include the same pertinent info such as web links, contact info and social media profile links. However, the difference is that Announcements are meant to be an occasional, brief communication that informs your audience of something special happening in your career. Perhaps it's a recent sale, a special commission, a review or critique in a magazine or media outlet, or the introduction to a new body of work.

I would suggest creating separate templates for each type of email communication (Newsletters, Invites, Announcements, and whatever else you choose to employ). Once you have a design you are comfortable with, stick with it for a period of time. This makes it simple for you, so you don't have to reinvent the wheel each time you send something out, and it makes it clear to your audience what they are receiving and who it is from. They will come to recognize your email communications just as they recognize their favorite brands in the marketplace.

On a final note, I will say that people will unsubscribe from your list occasionally, and it stings a little bit when they do. It's hard not to take it personally. One thing I tell myself to ease my hurt feelings is this: "The people who choose to leave are just making more room for the people who want to be here." Don't worry about the people who opt out; rather, concern yourself with providing continued value to those who stay engaged.

You can't please everybody—nor do you have to—so don't even bother trying. Just make sure you continue growing your list at every available opportunity.

3.6

Social Media

(Note to the Grammar Police: social media is plural for "social medium" and should be treated as a plural when writing about it. However, it feels weird to write "social media are" or to use "they" when referring to social media, which the casual reader may see as a typo. Therefore, writers often treat it as singular, even when we know we shouldn't. I will try to treat it properly in this section, but I may flip-flop. If so, please forgive.)

The numerous social networks that proliferate on the web have brought the far-reaching power of mass media to the consumer level. For the first time in history, any ordinary person can become their own multi-media powerhouse with the potential to reach a mass audience with a minimal investment of time and money. This is huge. I won't bother stating all the statistics that you might find in another book that is trying to sell you on the idea that social media is the greatest thing since sliced bread. The truth is that all these social platforms are just more tools for you to utilize in your marketing toolbox. But, as far as tools go, they are pretty awesome.

The biggest mistake people make when using social media for business is to assume that these platforms offer just another form of "push marketing," which is to say they simply use it to push marketing messages out as if it were a TV, a radio or a newspaper. Many marketers and "social media experts" hail social media as a marketing revolution, but I believe it's more of a communications revolution and should be treated as such. You need to engage your audience in a two-way dialogue and show your own personality, ideas and opinions while demonstrating that you are interested in and respect theirs as well.

Facebook

Currently, the granddaddy of all social platforms is Facebook. As of this writing, Facebook just celebrated its "One Billion Users" milestone, so you and everyone you know are probably already using FB for personal use. However, there is a difference between using it to further your art business and using it to tell us how tired you are, complain about the weather, or post yet another picture of your cat doing something silly. Sure, personal posts are the foundation of Facebook, but the most successful users find a way to strike that delicate balance of being personal AND professional.

As for myself, I often struggle with injecting a personal element because I truly love business and am not as interested in the random musings and everyday mundanities of the people I follow (nor am I that interested in sharing my own). But, as much as I love talking, reading, sharing and learning about the marketing business, not all my friends and followers share my fervent passion.

Therefore, in order to create engagement and nurture relationships, I need to occasionally post things that are personal and universal. Many people struggle with just the opposite, so when it comes time to amp up their art business, they feel awkward about soiling the waters with their "commercial" posts.

There are two routes you can take when using Facebook as a tool to further your art career: you can use your personal account and interject a small percentage of business (i.e., art) posts along with your personal posts, or you can set up a separate Business Page and intersperse a small percentage of personal posts along with your business posts. Let's take a look at both options.

Personal Profiles – If you do decide to simply use your personal Facebook profile as a tool to build awareness of your art, you really need to be aware of who your audience is and what your objective is. Here are some important questions to ask yourself:

- Are the people I'm friends with on Facebook truly interested in my art career?
- Will they engage with my art posts?
- Will they come to my shows and offer support?
- Are they the people who will be buying my art?
- What am I hoping to achieve by sharing my art with this audience?

If your Facebook friends consist of extended family members, co-workers, old high-school buddies, fellow artists and some random people you meet at parties and events, then you may not gain much traction from posting your art to your current Facebook account. But again, that all depends on your objective.

If, after pondering the above questions, you realize that you're simply trying to keep your FB friends abreast of what you're up to in the art world, then injecting the occasional art post into your personal news feed makes sense.

Business Pages – If, on the other hand, you are trying to build a following of art critics, collectors, gallery owners, fans and people who can open doors to exhibitions, sales and opportunities to further your art career, then it's better to set up a business page for your art business. Keep in mind that doing so requires extra effort to maintain activity on your page, actively seek out new fans to "like" your page, and continue to engage the audience you do accumulate.

Running a FB business page is similar to running a blog in that it takes time, effort and dedication to maintain activity. Otherwise, just like those millions of abandoned blogs floating around in cyberspace, your biz page may accrue several fans who "like" your page once but never return to engage with you or your content due to lack of consistent activity.

If you decide you're ready to set up your own business page, keep in mind you want to make it different enough from your personal account to warrant having two separate accounts. Therefore, really put on your Art-Business Hat when setting up your page. If your personal profile consists of your real name (e.g., Spencer McGee), then name your business page appropriately (e.g., Spencer McGee Fine Art). Refer back to the Naming section of this book for tips on effective naming strategies.

When it comes to filling out your page profile, there's an About section and a Description section. Use the information you crafted in the Right Message section and fill this in accordingly. If you want, you can use your Artist Statement for the Description section. Facebook Timeline allows you to upload a cover photo—a large, horizontal image that resides at the top of your page—in addition to your profile pic. People will see your cover photo only when they go directly to your page, but your profile pic will show up in their stream with every post or comment you make.

You can either use a photo of you, the artist, for your profile pic and have your cover photo represent your art, or use a picture of your art for your profile pic and include yourself in the cover photo. Either way, you should make yourself visible to your audience because we want to see the artist behind the work. When we see your creative expression, we want to form a visual of the human who is responsible for this expression. Don't attempt to hide behind your art, or make the mistake of feeling that you are too unworthy, unattractive or uninteresting to merit a photo of yourself. It's not about vanity, it's about human connection. People form emotional connections and bonds with other humans, and are more likely to stop and read a post or comment with your picture attached than they are when it's accompanied by a tiny thumbnail of your latest painting. You are one of a kind, so be proud of the unique, distinct, creative individual you are and show yourself to the world.

If you do decide to use a piece of your art for your profile pic, keep in mind that at 180 pixels square, the photo is too small to effectively showcase your work. Therefore be selective with the image you use. As a test, scroll through your Facebook newsfeed and note which photos catch your eye, and which ones you don't even notice. The trick here is to get noticed, which ultimately is the objective of every artist. Therefore choose a profile pic that stands out. The cover photo is a nice size for showing any photo that works well in the horizontal format. This could be a closeup detail shot of your latest piece, a wide shot of you working in your studio, a photo of your latest exhibit, or anything else that is representative of your art business or your creative process.

Photo Albums – With the launch of Timeline, Facebook has really evolved into a great visual medium that presents images in a beautiful way. The platform automatically organizes photos into albums that are easy to browse, share and comment on. You can access all your photos on the left dashboard of your home page. Any photo in which you are tagged is filtered into the "Photos of You" tab. Photos that you upload or share on your timeline are shown by clicking the tab simply called "Photos." Under the "Albums" tab, pictures are further filtered into various categories, including the specific albums you create.

You can create an album by uploading a batch of photos, name your album and add captions or descriptions to each photo. Albums are great for showcasing separate bodies of work, specific exhibitions, opening receptions, works-in-progress, or anything that you wish to curate and display in its own mini photo gallery. The key word here is "curate." I've seen many people take the lazy approach and upload 127 photos from an event, not even caring that their bloated batch contains poorly-lit shots, blurry pics, near-duplicates, and only a handful of what could be qualified as "good photos." Editing is a good skill to develop, which means you take the time to edit out the weak, sub-par or just plain bad photos, and attempt to covey your visual narrative using only a select grouping of the best photos. This makes for a much stronger, more compelling viewing experience.

I have sold art that someone discovered in one of my photo albums. I have also been contacted by a fraudulent scammer who discovered art in one of my photo albums. He sent an email stating his intent to purchase a piece that he listed by name. I had never heard of the guy, and for some reason felt skeptical, so I did a Google search on "his name+art." The search results turned up a blog post by a female artist who had also been contacted by this same guy, whom proceeded to suggest a complicated plan for the artist to ship the artwork and pick up a check from someone in the area, yada, yada. In other words, not every contact you make will be legit and you should not only proceed with caution, but also make sure your Facebook privacy settings are set in a way that makes you comfortable.

There are some gray areas when it comes to Facebook policies of content ownership, but the bottom line is once you upload anything, it exists on their servers, meaning they own it. Your goal should not be to build the Facebook brand and increase traffic for Zuckerberg, but rather build your own brand and drive traffic to your site. Therefore, think of Facebook as a teaser for your art. Don't give away the farm. Showcase just enough to get people interested and excited, then direct them to your site to experience the motherload of your creative expression.

Events – When it comes time to promote an art opening or other special occasion, you can create an Event with Facebook and invite your friends and followers to attend. This is another reason to make sure the people you are engaging on Facebook are interested in supporting you. Event invitations have become so ubiquitous that they can start to feel like spam. If you're still determining which of your friends and followers are likely to show up at your events, then be generous with your invites. Keep track of who is commenting on the Event wall, who is showing up to the actual event and which people seem genuinely interested in supporting what you're doing.

Once you've gathered this information, start getting more selective with your invites. It's both obvious and irritating when people create events and simply invite their entire Friend list without any consideration of logistics or interest. I moved from Minnesota to California in 2008 and I'm still getting invited to art shows and music gigs in Minnesota five years later! Uh, sorry folks, I will not be attending.

Facebook continues to improve its photo-viewing experience, so, while Event pages used to only allow small thumbnails, they now allow large, horizontal header images. When you create your event, upload a compelling photo to represent it, and take advantage of your available photo real estate. Fill in the required information fields as completely as possible, providing juicy, descriptive copy that makes it seem like people would really be missing out if they didn't attend.

You can even post photos and videos on the Event wall to build buzz and get people excited. Offering continual activity on the Event wall will offer a richer, multimedia experience for the viewers and encourage more engagement surrounding the Event.

Speaking of engagement, once people do start accepting, declining, waffling (the non-committal folks who select the "Maybe" option) and commenting, be sure you're there to comment, like, reply, answer questions and generally moderate the action on the wall. Don't simply create an Event, fire off a bulk invite and leave it at that. Instead, take advantage of every opportunity to build excitement, connections and conversation surrounding your event.

Facebook Content

Some may say that the absolute randomness of the platform is its greatest strength. Our minds and thoughts tend to be quite random and having a real-time tool that allows us to spew any old thought or idea out into the world is pretty cool. It's also pretty irritating. The proliferation of social networks has created a global society of junkies addicted to the dopamine rush of instant peer validation. We've become a mass of preening, narcissistic over-sharers who have come to believe every thought that pops into our heads is a witty, profound, undeniable nugget of brilliance worthy of broadcasting to everyone we've ever met.

Be that as it may, there are some strategic tips that will help you get the most out of this social network as a brand-building, art business tool. The general content and focus of your Facebook presence will depend on who you are, where your interests lie and how you choose to use the platform.

Of course you want to post personal or universal insights, but for effective business purposes, keep your overall content to a narrow, art-related focus. Create posts that will encourage likes, shares and comments by asking questions, soliciting opinions, or even prompting viewers to "Like" something as a response to a query or statement.

For example, if you can only submit one art piece to a group exhibit and you're undecided, post pictures of a couple of pieces and ask your audience to help you choose. If you come across a great artist, see a great exhibit, or discover a new gallery, share your discovery by posting a photo, link or comment. Including other people's work in your own field of focus will show that you're not simply a self-promotional artist (which is fine to an extent), but also a fan, a supporter, and an aficionado of all things art.

The best attribute of any social media platform is that it levels the playing field. Social platforms allow you a chance to connect, engage and converse with the people who can make a difference in your career. When you're seeking people to connect with and organizations to follow, seek out the players, the movers and shakers in the industry, the galleries, the critics, the bloggers, journalists and media personalities. This doesn't mean you have to pander, snivel and act like a boot-licking lackey to the stars of the art world. You can simply engage them on human terms based on your shared love of the creative arts, and let the relationship build naturally over time.

I have been accepted into an exhibit by posting an image of my work on a gallery's Facebook wall. I have also been rejected for an exhibit after posting an image of my work on a gallery's Facebook wall. Sometimes using Facebook in this manner will forge new relationships and connections and sometimes it will not. The fact that it is possible to use Facebook (and other social platforms) in this manner is pretty exciting and offers the potential to make your art-marketing endeavors a lot easier.

The staggering popularity of Facebook can lead people to believe that it's the all-knowing, all-powerful Oz of the social media marketing world. Keep in mind that Facebook is just one tool in your marketing communications toolbox, so don't get lazy and focus your sole efforts there. Experiment and discover other tools that work for you and use them all together in a cohesive, integrated way. Don't get overwhelmed and think you have to implement and maintain dozens of marketing tools and platforms. Pick three that meet your needs and start there. If that feels too comfortable, go ahead and select up to six. The idea is to increase and improve on what you've done in the past, without letting it interfere with the creation of your art, which is your top priority. You still want to be an artist who makes time for marketing rather than a marketer who tries to find time for art.

YouTube

Video is an excellent medium for visual artists and can be used in a variety of ways to educate, entertain and inform your audience. The low cost and easy accessibility of the tools necessary to create, edit and host video have made it a must-have medium that anyone can take advantage of. Before the explosion of YouTube, I was running a video production company in Minneapolis, and I spent thousands of dollars on a professional video camera and equipment, rental fees for production houses and editing studios, and payment for talent and crews. These days, I shoot video on my iPhone, edit with iMovie, upload to YouTube and call it a day. It's important to mention that YouTube is owned by Google, so you need to have a Gmail account in order to set up and sign in to your YouTube account.

Video Channels – YouTube allows you to create your own "channel" which, like every other social platform, you want to populate with a profile photo, general information (keeping your Right Message in mind), a link to your website, and a memorable name. The name is important because it becomes part of the URL that you will promote to drive people to your channel. For example, the channel I've created for Liberty Arts Gallery is youtube.com/libertyarts. You want the name to be short, intuitive, relevant and easy to remember, and it should contain either your own name, or your art-biz name (refer back to the Naming section of this book).

Since Google wants to create a seamless, integrated experience between all their products (namely Gmail, Google Plus and YouTube), they have recently initiated a push for YouTube channels (and their corresponding URLs) to be listed under your personal name (youtube.com/nikolasallen) rather than your business name (youtube.com/bamconsulting). It's not mandatory at this time, so you can still opt to ignore their request if you wish. My suggestion is to use the same name you've decided to use across all your other platforms.

The cool thing about channels is that they allow you to store and present all your videos in one place, so you can drive people to your channel, rather than sending them to a bunch of separate video links. YouTube channels allow you to present a professional-looking platform for your videos, and its user interface is beautiful and customizable, so you can tweak it to match your visual identity. I've said it before and I'll say it again: your entire online presence should have as much cohesion and consistency as possible—names, photos, descriptions, everything!

Video Camera – Almost every cell phone has a video camera function. Some are better than others, of course, but the popularity of user-generated content on platforms such as YouTube has lowered viewer expectations of quality and aesthetic since the days when, say, David Coverdale's girlfriend was rolling around on the hood of a car in the latest Whitesnake video.

Almost all digital cameras have video functions as well, even the cheapest point-and-shoot ones. You can even create videos from the webcam on your computer monitor and upload directly to Facebook and YouTube. If you want to take it up a notch, you can purchase a HD digital video camera on Amazon.com for under $200.

My mantra is this: use the tools you've got. Don't wait until you can afford the latest and greatest equipment; start shooting on your phone or your cheap camera and get the hang of the medium while you start crafting your own style. The important thing is that you must be able to off-load the footage quickly and easily, so you can perfect your system of shoot, edit, upload, repeat.

Video Editing – YouTube has a basic video editor that allows you to upload raw video footage then trim it, add titles, transitions and background music. Both Macs and PCs come with native video editing programs such as iMovie and Movie Maker respectively, and a Google search for "free video editing software" turns up a host of available options for both Mac and PC. Any one of these basic programs will suffice for the job at hand. There will be a learning curve, but once you get the hang of your program of choice, editing your videos will become easier and will give them a polished and professional look that is impressive to the viewer.

While we're discussing editing, let's talk about video length. Most people have a tendency to drag their videos out too long, and in our attention-deficit society, that's the kiss of death. It's crazy how loooooong even a five-minute video feels when you're watching on your phone or computer screen, especially if it's just a person talking to the camera. I believe the sweet spot to be about 2–3 minutes long. If you love good TV commercials like I do, you'll know that a great story can be told in 30 seconds. And, if you're a music fan, you'll know that the best pop songs clock in at about two-and-a-half minutes. Keep this in mind when you're making your own videos. It's better to produce lots of short, concise videos that hold the attention of your audience rather than having them click off halfway through your six-minute video.

Search Engine Optimization (SEO) – Okay, your video is shot, edited and uploaded, now let's make sure it's easy to find. Knowing what words and phrases your audience is using to find artists in your category will help your videos show up in their searches. Try to use these keywords in the following places

- **Video Titles** – Keep your titles short and snappy. They should tease, entice, and provide a glimpse of what benefit awaits the viewer. Similar to your email marketing subject lines, you want to craft concise, descriptive video titles that are too compelling to pass up.

- **Video Description** – The first thing that should go in the description box on every video is your Web site URL. In order to make it clickable, include the "http://www." When your video is viewed on YouTube or Facebook, or it shows up on a Google search results page, it will be accompanied by its title and description. Therefore, you want your Web address to be visible right away. Beyond that, create a keyword-rich description that sums up your video's content. Remember, you're still writing for humans, so make it coherent, while including the pertinent Who, What, Where details.

- **Keywords Field** – Under the Video Description box is a Keywords field. As mentioned above, keywords are important to think about at all times, but this field is where you can really pack them in. There is a limit as to how many you can enter. They don't make it clear what the limit is, but they do let you know when you've exceeded it. So, stick to a focused list of words and phrases such as "fine art paintings, videos about art, watercolor lessons with [your name], pop artist Chicago," etc. You definitely want to include your name, your city or town, your state, and your creative category in the keywords. This way, your videos will not only show up in searches people do directly on YouTube, but they will also show up when people do Google searches that include those related keywords. Your goal is to make it very easy for people to find you online via your website, your social media platforms and your videos.

Video Content

In the world of internet marketing, they say "Content is king." After all, if you're creating a video channel, you obviously need to produce plenty of content to share with your audience. As with blogging and any other social media efforts, a brief flurry of activity followed by lengthy idle spells will not help you build a loyal audience of engaged fans. It will be up to you to build upon the subjects, concepts and themes of your videos to create a wealth of content that keeps your viewers coming back for more.

The following ideas should help get the ball rolling:

Studio Footage – It's always fun to see where the magic happens for an artist. Whether you're giving a video tour, or using your studio as the backdrop while you discuss your latest project, allowing viewers to see your creative space offers a fun, intimate glimpse into your world.

Art Opening Footage – Shoot video footage at your own art openings, get video testimonials from visitors, and if you're giving a short talk or presentation about your work, have a friend capture it for you. You can also shoot footage at other art openings you attend, but you want to be careful—some artists don't want you shooting their work, and some galleries have a no camera policy.

Interviews – Whether you are in front of the camera or behind it, video interviews with you or with other interesting creative people, gallery owners or collectors can offer a wealth of great content that is informational and educational as well as entertaining.

Making-Of Videos – One of my Facebook friends is an artist who produces intricate, hand-drawn mandalas, and she produces amazing time-lapse videos of herself creating the pieces. This produces a lot of footage, because you have to shoot the whole process then speed up the video. Another option is to shoot a little footage at each progressive stage of your artwork's creation. This gives greater insight into your process and it's always fascinating for viewers to see the work that went into your finished art pieces.

How-To Tips – One artist who has really impressed me with her online presence is Lori McNee (you can find her on Twitter @ lorimcneeartist). Not only has she perfected her craft, but she has parlayed her skills into a business by offering "Fine art tips, business and social media advice for aspiring and professional artists." If you specialize in certain areas of expertise that will benefit others, sharing your knowledge via educational, informational how-to videos will provide much value to your audience, which is always one of your top objectives when it comes to any social media activity.

There are many types of videos you can create, so use these content ideas as a starting point. Eventually, you will discover the types of videos you enjoy making—and your audience enjoys viewing—and you can narrow your focus. Until then, experiment with new things and have fun.

Spreading the Word

Once you've got a few videos on your YouTube channel, promote it on all of your marketing collateral: include the URL in your email signature and your e-newsletter, post videos on Facebook and your blog, tweet links to your videos, and take every opportunity to direct your audience there. Try to keep track of audience feedback and engagement levels to see what's working and what's not. Making videos is a decent amount of work, so you want to make sure you enjoy the process, AND that your audience is deriving some benefits from your efforts. Remember, even when it comes to video—it's about them, not you.

Twitter

When it comes to determining which social platforms to use for business, Twitter is the one people seem to resist the most. Either they just don't get it (when you see someone's tweet stream for the first time, it does look a bit like hieroglyphics), or they question the validity of the medium. The truth is, it's just another tool, and just like every marketing tool, it's not mandatory for everybody—or every business.

Traditional thinking states that marketing tools should directly affect sales and produce measurable results. When it comes to social media marketing tools, that way of thinking—while certainly valid and legitimate—does not quite apply as it once did. Many people have taken up Twitter for business with hopes to immediately increase sales revenue. Unfortunately, that approach is almost guaranteed to disappoint.

Some people claim Twitter is a great conversational tool, but I disagree. Very often, when you tweet at someone, pose a question or send a direct message (DM), it takes hours or days before you get a reply. And, whereas Facebook keeps conversations in a tidy, threaded comment stream under each post, replies on Twitter get thrown into the ongoing rush of your tweet stream, which is nearly impossible to keep up with. You do get notified when people reply, re-tweet, or use your user name (@YourName) in a tweet, but as far as conversations go, it's a disjointed process at best.

Personally, I love Twitter. I don't own a TV, so it becomes my go-to source for breaking news. The real-time nature of the platform means people are tweeting about hot topics long before they hit the airwaves of traditional media. It's also great for educational purposes. People in every industry are tweeting links to blog posts, articles, white papers, ebooks, and everything else that will help you keep up with the latest happenings in your field of interest.

And, of course, I use Twitter to share my own blog posts and activities, as well as links to articles, posts and videos that my audience might enjoy. This helps build my reputation as a thought leader in the field of marketing, which establishes credibility and attracts clients. You can do the same in the art field.

All of the same rules and principles we've discussed throughout the book (provide value to your audience, don't make it all about you, keep your activity consistent, etc.) apply to Twitter as well.

If you decide you want to commit to using Twitter as a tool in your art-marketing strategy, the following tips will help you get the most out of the platform:

11 Best-Practice Twitter Tips:

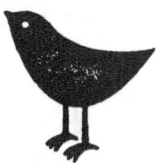

- Use a bold, eye-catching profile pic that will stand out in the tweet stream.

- Create a @UserName that's easy to read, understand and remember (@yourname, @yourartbizname, etc.).

- Fill out the profile completely (use Right Message) and include a link to your website in the profile.

- Customize the background and color palette to match your consistent online identity.

- Upload photos of your art, your studio, fun events and interesting people in your circle to fill out your photo slideshow area.

- Go on a mad spree of following people, organizations and publications in the Arts industry (the more people you follow, the more people will reciprocate).

- Keep to a narrow, art-related focus with your tweets.

- Inject some personal quips, thoughts or status updates to humanize your activity.

- Tweet occasional links that drive traffic to your website, blog or other social channels.

- Engage your followers by retweeting (RT) their posts, mentioning them (include @TheirName in your tweet), and sending the occasional DM (Direct Message).

- DO NOT automate your DMs (e.g., setting up an automatic Direct Message that goes to everyone who follows you). This shows poor etiquette, yet tons of people still do it.

By using Twitter, I have earned opportunities to write guest blog posts, been interviewed for people's websites, communicated with gallery owners, and generally made some cool connections that wouldn't have been otherwise possible. So the platform is clearly useful for those who use it properly. The downside is that it can be a tremendous time-suck, just like any social platform. If you do decide to implement Twitter, make sure you are disciplined with your time spent there, so the results you achieve are proportionate to the effort expended.

Pinterest

A relatively new platform, Pinterest launched in March 2010 and was devised as an "online pinboard to share and organize things you love." In December 2011, traffic to the site skyrocketed and it officially became one of the major players in the social photo-sharing game. The site stayed hot throughout 2012, which had marketers salivating and falling all over themselves in a mad rush to capitalize on the new phenomenon.

The problem was that, regardless of all the new "Pinterest For Business" books that were coming out (prematurely, in my opinion), most of the visitors were not using the site as a shopping portal. According to Anika Burke, owner of Anika Burke's Eclectic Boutique in Chico, California, and an early adopter of Pinterest, "People do not come to Pinterest to be marketed to, they just want to find cool stuff and have fun. I think of my Pinterest boards as my 'Dream Book,' a place where I post my ideas, inspirations and wants."

That all being said, most of the photos posted on Pinterest contain links to other websites, and recent studies have shown that Pinterest has emerged as a major source of traffic to those sites. While some visitors surely end up making a purchase from (e-commerce) sites they visit via Pinterest, a large percentage of them are still just browsing and exploring. Since it is a photo-centric platform, Pinterest is perfect for visual artists. Whether your objective is to "find cool stuff and have fun" like Anika Burke does, drive traffic back to your own site, or simply use it as an online scrapbook, these now-familiar tips will help you optimize your Pinterest presence.

User Name – We've talked about user names above, so the same rules apply here. Many Pinterest users simply use their full name on their profile (Your Name), and a variation of that for their User Name, which becomes the URL people type in to find you (pinterest.com/yourname). If you share the same name as another Pinterest user, or your name is long or hard to pronounce, you may use a variation for your User Name (pinterest.com/y_name). If you choose to use your art biz name as your Profile Name (Red Robot Studios) or your User Name (pinterest.com/redrobotstudios), be sure to include your personal name in the profile bio (e.g., Robotic Metal Sculpture by Rob Otto). This will help humans and search engines find you based on your name, which is important if they don't know your business name.

Profile – As with all social platforms, your profile contains a photo thumbnail, a short bio and links to your other online properties. The photo is small and square, so use something bold and recognizable that stands out. One thing I should note is that it's okay to use the same headshot or profile pic across all your social platforms. If you're like Lady Gaga or Nicky Minaj and look drastically different in every picture, you obviously wouldn't even think of doing that. However, creating a uniform look across all mediums is a great way to build a recognizable identity and consistent brand, which is a key objective for any business.

Keep your bio short and concise, using rich, descriptive keywords while keeping your Right Message in mind. Fill in the links to your website and other social media platforms, which creates an interconnected web across your entire online presence.

Boards – Pinterest boards are similar to Facebook photo albums in that you can organize multiple images based around a particular topic. Try to create individual pinboards with clearly separate categories so you don't spend a lot of time wondering where your images should go when it's time to post. On every social platform, it's considered poor etiquette to only post, link, pin and tweet about your own stuff, so make sure your boards contain a healthy mixture of photos by other people in addition to your own.

For example, you could create a board named "Artists I Love," "Crazy-Awesome Designers" or "Inspiring Photographers" and post images you come across that fall into that category. For your own boards, you could name them "Artwork in Progress," "My Latest Paintings" or "Recent Gallery Shows" and pin photos of your own into each category. When pinning photos, you can add a description as well as a link to the location on the web where they reside.

If you post a photo by an inspiring photographer, be sure to both give credit by listing their name in the description, and link the photo to their website so other people can explore that artist further if they're interested. Likewise, when you pin your own art, do the same with a short yet detailed description and a link back to your website.

Search – When naming your boards and writing your photo descriptions, keep SEO in mind. When Pinterest first emerged, its search capabilities were lacking. While this has surely improved over the past year, it's still not the key feature of the platform. Therefore, make sure you think about how people are looking for things when they're on the site and work those keywords into your copywriting.

It's helpful to do some testing of your own. Type some keywords and phrases that interest you into the search bar and see what comes up. Notice how other users have used keywords to get noticed and follow suit with your own pins and boards.

Get Social – Keep in mind that Pinterest is a social platform, which means you should interact with and engage other users both reactively and proactively. The idea is to discover other users who are pinning things you find interesting and Like, Comment, Repin and Follow—actions that should be familiar if you are using other social platforms. Other users will do the same with your pins, which allows your art to potentially reach a wider audience. And, just in case you haven't been paying attention, that's the whole point!

Instagram

Instagram is photo-sharing service that allows users to take photos and share them on a variety of social networking platforms, including its own. Instagram's unique difference was originally its filter feature, which allows users to apply fun filters their photos, which adds an "artistic" flair and produces moody results. However, the filter feature has been adopted by other models, so it's not so unique anymore.

Instagram's real claim to fame is its acquisition by Facebook for $1 billion in cash and stock in 2012. Several months after the purchase Instagram went from being a mobile-only platform to allowing users to create an online portal they can access from a computer, which looks a lot like the Facebook Timeline design.

Not too long after the acquisition, outrage erupted when Instagram changed their Terms of Policy to include language that seemed to allow them to sell users' photos to businesses and other entities without giving any compensation to the people who took the pictures. This change supported the stance of corporate parent Facebook, which feels that "whatever you upload to our site is OURS." The backlash caused Instagram CEO Kevin Systrom to issue a public apology and vow to rework the language of the new Terms. As with all legal-speak, the Terms are still pretty gray, so proceed at your own risk.

As for using the platform, many of the above rules and strategies apply regarding your user name, profile picture and description. The same social nomenclature of Like, Share, Comment and Follow is used, as well as the etiquette surrounding engagement with other users. As for content ideas, you can also use those discussed above, or you can post something ongoing like "A Day in the Life of an Artist," and vow to post one picture per day that relates to your world.

You can Tag your photos, which is similar to Facebook and alerts the person or company you tagged, and you can add Captions and #Hashtags to your photos, which are searchable and will help your content get found. Unlike Pinterest, the photos on Instagram do not contain outbound links, so they cannot be used to drive traffic to other online properties. Therefore, this platform should only be considered if connecting with your audience through visual storytelling is a priority that will benefit both parties. Remember, there are many tools available and only so much time to use them well, so select the tools in your marketing toolbox wisely.

Social Media Summary

While the available social media platforms each have different interfaces, strengths, weaknesses and levels of popularity, the general concepts, strategies and Best Practices that should be applied to each are all pretty similar. This is actually a relief. After all, it can get pretty overwhelming to think you have to maintain a presence on all these platforms, so it's nice to know you don't have reinvent the wheel each time you adopt a new one.

Also, you may notice that in the above section, I chose not to delve too deeply into the technical, step-by-step "how-to" of setting up your social profiles.

I made this decision for several reasons:

1) The focus of this book is a macro view of the big-picture **strategy** of a fully-integrated marketing plan, which is often overlooked and, in my opinion, more essential than step-by-step instructions for implementing new tools.

2) There are plenty of other books and resources available that focus on the technical aspect of each of the aforementioned platforms.

3) The features and interfaces of all these tools are constantly evolving and changing (Facebook is notorious for continually tinkering with their platform), which renders certain information obsolete at a rapid pace.

My intention is to include and explain enough information to help you choose the right tools and get you started with your strategy. You may discover that you need to seek further resources, or employ the "learn by doing" technique for some of the practical mechanics of these tools, and that's to be expected. Education is an ongoing endeavor that is always available to those who continue to seek it.

3.7

Printed Collateral

In order to maximize the effectiveness of your art-marketing efforts, you must maintain a balanced focus between your online and your offline presence. The internet is great for allowing you to cultivate your online brand, but in order to bring a sense of truth, reality and integrity into your virtual existence, you need to make your mark out in the physical world. You've heard me mention consistency several times, and never is it more important to be consistent than when bridging your online and offline identities.

"Be Consistent: You've spent a lot of [time and] money on your name, website and logo. Are you using them consistently across the web, business cards, signage and even in your invoices/receipts? Take a 360 degree view of your business from your customers' eyes and make sure your hard-earned identity is served up consistently."

– Kevin Dougan, Strategic Public Relations

The visual elements of your business identity that Kevin mentions above all have the responsibility of conveying your image, your reputation and your brand to the world. In his book *BrandSimple*, Allen P. Adamson refers to these as branding signals. He explains:

"Branding signals are external and obvious things like logos and names, colors, signage, typefaces, images and promotions, package designs, and distribution channels. A good branding signal conveys the promise of a brand idea."

Way back in the Right Message section, we discussed your business name, which Adamson considers to be "one of the most critical of all branding signals." Hopefully you've given it plenty of consideration, because your name is really your starting point as we delve deeper into creating consistent offline marketing materials. Keep in mind that your materials may differ depending on your specific creative field and your needs. You also may discover some promotional tools that we don't cover here. Consider the following items as a starting point and continue to use those that produce results.

Creating Your Business Logo

Once you've decided on what name you'll be using for your art business, you'll want to create a logo and use that logo consistently on EVERY single piece of collateral you create. You can create a logo yourself, if you possess the skills and resources, or you can hire a graphic designer to design one for you. These days, you can't throw a tomato in a crowded room without hitting a graphic designer, so it should be easy to find one who will work within your budget.

Optionally, there are many online sites that offer logo design. Some of them are do-it-yourself sites and others offer the option to have several designers create a variety of proofs for you to choose from. Prices can range from $99 to $500 or more, so choose carefully in an effort to maximize your investment by getting the best design at an affordable price.

Whoever you decide to hire, make sure you see their portfolio first and ask for references. If they have a good working reputation and a decent selection of styles and designs that may align to the concept of your brand, give 'em a shot.

Choosing Your Weapons

Depending on the type of creative field you are in, the offline branding signals and marketing materials you utilize are going to differ:

- Artists may have portfolios, bios, artist statements, business cards, postcards, mailing labels, invoices, receipts, inventory lists, contracts, etc.

- Photographers and graphic designers may have portfolios, business cards, postcards, invoices, receipts, model releases, contracts, resumes, etc.

- Musicians may have CDs, DVDs, promo reels or CD samplers, press kits, biz cards, bios, flyers, posters, newsletters, stickers, apparel, contracts, etc.

- You may have even have a brick and mortar storefront, gallery or studio, which might include interior and exterior signage, bags, business cards, bookmarks, wrapping paper, stickers, mailing labels and all the necessary items utilized in retail.

While I won't go into detail about each piece, I will outline a few of the essential promo materials that every artist should be utilizing. Once you determine and design the look you want your identity to convey, it's a matter of adapting that look to each of the various sizes and formats of the individual pieces mentioned above.

Here are some primary things to consider when creating your visual identity in order to be consistent:

Color – Pick up to three colors to use across your whole identity. Even just one color can be effective (think H&R Block green, IBM blue, Coca-Cola red). Usually, more than three is overkill and often looks amateur. Using different shades, tints, hues or percentages of the same color is a nice way to add variety while keeping things consistent.

If you're printing your collateral at a print shop on a traditional printing press (unless your uncle owns a shop, or you're part of the hand-made Makers Movement, the probability of this is pretty low these days), the more colors you use, the more expensive it will be—and it can get quite spendy. So keep that in mind when choosing the color(s) to represent your brand identity. However, more and more companies are now printing digitally and can produce full-color pieces (what's known traditionally as 4-color process) at surprisingly affordable prices. In the name of consistency (and there's a high margin of inconsistency and color variation when it comes to printing), try to get as much of your collateral as you can printed at the same company.

While your offline branding signals will often be printed either using Pantone colors (PMS), or process colors (CMYK), your online identity will be represented with RGB (Red, Green, Blue) colors. RGB colors are created by the light-emitting diodes of your screen or monitor, which can create bright, vibrant colors that look great on-screen, but cannot be duplicated by the inks used in the printing process. So, when creating your identity, be sure to choose colors that will replicate both on-screen and off. I recommend starting with your offline materials, and converting the design for web use, rather than the other way around.

Fonts – As with colors, you also want to minimize the amount of fonts you use for your identity. I got a postcard in the mail recently for an art opening and EVERY bit of information was printed in a different font. I counted eighteen different fonts on one postcard! Some people may think this looks "artsy" or "whimsical," but it can also look disjointed, unfocused and confused.

There's really no reason to use more than three fonts. Perhaps that includes one serif font (serifs are the little "feet" at the base of each letter in fonts like Times New Roman, Palatino and Courier), one strong sans serif font (font without serifs, or "feet," such as Helvetica, Arial and Franklin Gothic) and, optionally, one fun, "designy" font (e.g., grunge, script, or retro groovy) used sparingly. I like to mix serif with sans serif, using one for headlines and subheads and one for body copy. Another option is to pick one font that has a lot of styles (Regular, Italic, Bold, Bold Italic, Narrow, Black), like Franklin Gothic, and use a combination of its various styles.

There are tons of great fonts available out there (see Resources section), which makes it difficult to narrow it down to the select few that best represent your brand. Some of the coolest fonts are grungy, distorted, industrial and edgy, but also very difficult to read. Other fonts are very dated, and immediately conjure up a specific era. This can be a good or a bad thing depending on what you're going for. I can't look at a grunge font today without it bringing me back to the '90s, which is when they came into vogue. Same with certain techno-looking fonts that came of age with DJ culture in the '00s.

That being said, sometimes those fonts are exactly what work for a design or an identity, so take the time to choose fonts that truly represent you and your art. When in doubt, go with the classics and choose something that will have a shelf life.

The key point is to make your collateral legible. No matter how cool a font looks, if people can't read it, it's not serving its main purpose. Before you print up your entire branding identity, get other people's opinions. Show them your ideas and designs (TIP: posting them to your social platforms with a request for feedback and opinions is a good way to create engagement), and if more than one person says your fonts are hard to read, reconsider your font choice. Don't make the mistake of sacrificing function for form. Choose your fonts wisely and use them consistently across all your branding signals.

Business Cards

The most common item listed above is the business card. Even in the age of the smartphone, I feel that everybody should have a business card. It's a pocket-size advertisement for who you are, what you do and how to reach you. Therefore, it needs to look good. Sure, those free VistaPrint business cards that so many artists seem to love are quick and easy, but they scream, "Amateur!" Avoid the temptation to just go for the cheapest solution, and instead be willing to spend $60 to print a box of 500 great-looking cards.

You should be selective with the information you put on your card. I've seen cards that list company phone numbers, 1-800 numbers, direct lines, cell phones, pagers, emails, faxes, websites, blogs, social networks, yada, yada, yada. This is overkill. Giving too many options makes contacting someone seem like an overwhelming chore. However, there are several things your business card should include. Pick and choose what's appropriate for you from the following list of items:

Your Logo – Whether this is a logo for your personal name or the name of your company, if you have a logo, it should be featured prominently.

Your Name – This is a no-brainer. When networking, people want to know who you are.

Your Title or What You Do – This is optional. However, when that Gallery Director you schmoozed at the opening pulls a stack of biz cards out of her pocket after a night of networking—especially if the booze was flowing—your title or specialty will remind her WHY she got your card in the first place and HOW your specialty will help meet her objectives.

Your Contact Info – What's your MAIN preferred method of contact? If it's email, include ONE email address. It's acceptable not to include your phone number if you don't want to, because electronic communication is the norm these days. However, if you do choose to include your number, just use your ONE primary contact number.

> *Side Note:* The minute you give out your phone number, that phone becomes a business phone. Keep that in mind when you're answering unfamiliar numbers and be professional. Also, leave an outgoing message that speaks to your business or specialty, so if potential clients get your voicemail, they'll know that a) they've reached the right person, and b) you're a professional.

Your Address – This is ONLY necessary if you have a storefront, or if you send and receive lots of business-related mail. If neither of these applies to you, then do not put your address on your card, and instead, give it out on an as-needed basis.

Your Web URL – (By the way, URL stands for Uniform Resource Locator and is basically the "address" on the web where your site "lives.") Your website is where people will be able to view your art, learn more about you and your work, connect with you and do business with you. Your web address is often the main point of interest to people collecting your card, so it obviously needs to be on there—and on every other piece of collateral you create.

> *Side Note:* On PRINTED materials, we are well past the days of having to include "http://" in our web addresses. In fact, due to the public awareness of websites, it's even okay to omit the "www." In many cases, you can simply include, "yoursite. com", or "facebook.com/yourname" and people will get it. However, on some print materials I design for myself and clients, I will occasionally still include the "www." simply for aesthetic reasons, because it balances out the ".com" on the other side of the domain name.

On the WEB, you still must use "http://" if you want to create a clickable link. The "www." is often not needed, as browsers now know that this is part of every address on the "world-wide web," but again sometimes it's best to include just to be certain your browser knows where to go. It's a good idea to test every link you create on your website, your emails or your social media profiles, in order to be certain they go where they're supposed to go. It's quite frustrating to send out a newsletter to your entire list, only to later discover that the link you included only leads to a '404 – Page Not Found' error. Trust me, I've done it. Test, test, then test again.

Your Social Media URLs – This is optional and depends on whether you are using social media for business or for keeping in touch with friends and family. If you have a presence dedicated to your art business on any of the platforms we discussed above, include the URL on your card. If your social media presence is more of an outlet to post party pics and discuss the weather, food, how busy you are and other mundanities of life, then don't bother including your social media URLs on your printed business collateral.

An Image – (Optional) An image could enhance your card and make it stand out. If you're a visual artist, you may wish to show a piece of your work on your card. There's a great printing website called MOO.com that allows you to buy a box of custom business cards with different images on the back of EACH card. That's a great (and affordable) way to get your work out there and turns your box of biz cards into a mini portfolio.

Only for the bold: you could optionally include a picture of yourself on your card. If done right, this is a good way to personalize your card and allow people to recognize and remember who you are. If done wrong, well, you may end up being mistaken for a real estate agent. Remember, competition is fierce in this massive marketplace and the more ways you can get the attention of your market and stand out (positively) in the mind of your audience, the better.

QR Codes

You've probably seen those boxy graphic symbols on print advertisements, promotional materials and product packaging and wondered what the heck they were. They are called QR codes, which stands for Quick Response codes, and when used right, they can create deeper engagement with a smartphone-toting audience. QR codes are a bridge between the offline world and the online world. They could be mentioned in different areas of this book, but I have placed them among the printed promotional items because that is the most typical place you will use them.

Here's how they work:
First, you determine what web content or activity you want to provide via your QR code. You could link the code to videos, a specific section of your website (providing your site is mobile-optimized), your social media profiles, an email list sign-up form, etc.

Next, you create a QR code that will drive people to your web link. A Google search for "qr code generator" turns up many options. Some are quick and simple and others offer more advanced customization. I suggest you check out a few of the results listed on the first page of your search in order to see what these generators are all about, then choose one that seems easy and user-friendly to you. Follow the steps in your chosen QR code generator to create and download your code.

Your code becomes a graphic file that you can place on any print materials you want to. Since you've already determined how you want to use it, you should have an idea of where you want to implement it. For example, you could place it on your business card and link to the portfolio page of your site, or print it on a postcard and link to a video to provide a rich-media experience. When your audience comes into contact with your QR code, be it on your biz card, postcard or gallery title tag, they scan the code with their smartphone, which links them to your target destination. First, they must have a smartphone, not just a cell phone, and secondly, they must have a QR code reader, which they can download for free from any app store.

People seem to have a love/hate relationship with QR codes, but it's not the code itself that people find maddening (aside from people thinking they look ugly), but rather the useless way that unsavvy marketers are employing them. Some companies are using this technology in creative and innovative ways, while many others are turning people off to the whole idea of QR codes. The offenses range from simply sending people to the home page of a company website that is not even mobile-optimized, to creating a non-user-friendly mobile experience (fill out these 18 text fields to join our mailing list!), to putting QR codes on billboards (do you really want people trying to scan a billboard while driving?).

When using QR codes, the rules of creating Value and Engagement are important to keep in mind here. Don't just send people to your site; try to provide deeper, exclusive content, entertainment, information or special offers to people who interact with your QR codes. Also, keep your Right Message in mind and craft a Call to Action that lets people know what to do, and what they can expect from doing it. There's nothing enticing about seeing a naked QR code with no explanation of what it is, what it does, and why you should bother scanning it.

To promote one of the exhibits at Liberty Arts, I produced a short video of the artists talking about the work they created for the show. I created a QR code that linked to the video and placed the code on the back of the promo postcard. People who got the card could scan the code with their smartphones and watch the video, which added an extra layer of intrigue, excitement, and interactivity. I also embedded the same QR code in a photo of the artists that I submitted to local newspapers with a press release. Both of the newspaper editors replied immediately inquiring about the QR code, and we received coverage from both papers.

Postcards

Postcards are impactful, affordable and collectible marketing tools that can be used for many different purposes. There are different sizes available, but 4" × 6" and 5" × 7" are the sizes used most often. You can download appropriate templates from the website of the online printing service you will be using, as they provide complete guidelines for text placement, bleed area, trim size, etc.

There are also certain guidelines required by the U.S. Postal Service if you will be mailing the cards, so if you're planning an elaborate card or a large quantity, it's best to check with the post office before printing, so your card is in compliance. It sounds like a hassle, but once you become familiar with the print templates and postal guidelines, it becomes easier to produce future cards.

As for content, it depends on the usage of the postcard, but I always like to maximize the front real estate with one great image. Sure, you can include 2–3 images if you want, but keep it cohesive. I've seen artists try to cram lots of tiny pictures, text and information on the front, which is never as impactful as treating the front as a mini billboard with a strong image and minimal text.

Opening Night Invites – The primary use of postcards is to promote the opening of a show. In this case, the pertinent info you want to include is Who, What, When and Where. As I mentioned, the front of the card should contain an arresting image that catches the viewer's attention. If you include text on the front, perhaps it's the name of the gallery and the name of the show. As for the details, that's what the backside is for. Get their attention with the front, and make 'em flip the card over to learn more. The formula I've used for the front-side text on over 100 postcards I've designed is: "Gallery Name presents: Exhibit Name." If I want to expound, I'll include the tagline for the show: "Underwater Photography by Artist Name."

Then, on the back you include a short description of the exhibit or event (What), a brief mention of the artist (Who), dates and times of the event (When), and location and contact info for the venue (Where). Choose whether you want to include contact info for the gallery OR the artist. Of course, if you include contact info for the artist, make sure your website is listed, so each postcard acts as a traffic-driving promotion for your site.

Be sure to leave enough room for an address label on the right side if you plan on sending your cards through the mail. One final bit of info you may want to include on the back is a copyright or credit line referencing the photo shown on the front. You will notice that the real estate on the back of a postcard fills up very quickly.

One trick I use is to run the copyright in a vertical line between the left-hand content side of the card and the right-hand address side of the card. This allows you to get the extra info on the card and gives you a visual delineation between the content and the address. The wording I use is:

FRONT IMAGE: "Title of Piece" ©YEAR Artist Name

Thank You Cards – Sending hand-written Thank You cards on your own custom postcards is a great way to keep your art—and your exquisite manners—top of mind with people who are important to you and your career. With online digital printing, you can produce short print runs in quantities as low as 50. Unlike your Opening Reception postcards, on which you fill up the left side with pre-printed information about the show, your

Thank You cards should look more like traditional postcards you find in gift shops and truck stops.

These should contain a great shot of your work on the front (a message is optional but not necessary), and a little blurb about the artist at the top left side on the back. At the end of the blurb, be sure to include a call to action to visit your website (in case you haven't figured it out yet, your website should be listed on every single marketing tool you employ), and you can use the vertical copyright line idea I mentioned in the previous section to provide more info about the art piece(s) featured on the front. Otherwise, the backside is blank so you can write custom notes as needed.

The more Thank You cards you send, the more your art—even a tiny, 4" × 6" version of it—is out in the world. Consider the following recipients and reasons for sending your custom Thank You cards:

- Gallery directors, for accepting your work in a show
- Gallery directors, for considering but rejecting your work (leave them with a positive impression and they'll be happy to consider you in the future)
- Friends and family who come to your opening
- Journalists who give you press
- Bloggers who mention or cover the show
- Musicians or DJs who play at your openings
- Vendors who help you prepare for your show (printers, frame shop owners, art supply store employees, etc.)
- Anyone else who helps you hang, promote or otherwise set up or prepare for the show

What this means is that you have to actively seek out the physical addresses of each of these persons in order to send a postcard through the mail to them. It will be easy to find some of their addresses with a quick Google search, while gleaning other addresses maybe a bit more challenging—as people are more and more protective of their contact info. Don't be afraid to collect the business cards of everyone you deal with when preparing for an exhibit. If their address is not on their cards, you can always ask, "If I sent you something through the mail, where would I send it?" They may or may not give out an address, and if not, hey, at least you tried. In lieu of a postcard, you can still send them a Thank You email after the fact, which is recommended etiquette; it's just not quite as meaningful as a written card.

New Works Notice – No matter what size your body of work is, people are always curious to know, "What's next?" Producing small-batch runs of postcards that showcase new art pieces, a new series or a new medium is a great way to keep your target audience up to date on your ongoing creative evolution.

In the Ideal Audience section of this book, we discussed creating a contact list for the galleries in your chosen cities where you would like to exhibit your work. These galleries are prime candidates to receive ongoing communication from you regarding your evolving body of work. This is especially true if you have already reached out to them and they responded positively. However, even if they rejected an earlier submission—or you didn't hear back from them—curators and gallery directors are always interested in considering exciting, relevant work for future exhibits. Unless they explicitly ask you to cease communicating with them, continue to do so with notices of new work.

You should also send New Works Notices to previous buyers of your work, curators and directors at galleries where you have previously shown your work, any journalists, art critics, or bloggers who have written about you in the past (regardless of whether their mentions were positive or negative), and anyone in your local, personal or immediate circle who has shown consistent support of you and your art career.

In terms of design, New Works Notices should be similar to the Thank You cards described above. Photo(s) of the new work should adorn the front and a descriptive blurb about the new piece, series or medium should be printed on the top left-hand side of the back. You can even include the phrase "New Works by Artist Name" either on the front or prefacing the descriptive blurb on the back, to ensure that your recipients know what they are looking at.

Think about your Call to Action as well. What is it you want them to do when they get your postcard? Contact you? Visit your website? At the end of your descriptive blurb, include a concise sentence that tells them what they should do next. Be sure to leave space on the left side for a hand-written note, so you can add a personal touch that will assure your recipient that you're not just spamming every gallery with cards.

When I was working in the advertising industry in Minneapolis, I was responsible for hiring talent for photo shoots and ad campaigns. Photographers and model agencies were great about regular communication via postcards and promo packets showcasing new works or new headshots. I would keep their submissions in a file, which would be the first place I would look when it came time to produce a new shoot. Oftentimes, I hired those who had made the effort to stay on my radar, not only because they possessed the appropriate talent for the job, but also because they had made it easy for me to view, consider and contact them when it was time for action.

The same concept applies to galleries. When it comes time to flesh out the exhibition schedule for a new year, the curators are hungry for exciting work that will help them create a great schedule. By keeping in touch and showcasing your works, your name will be top-of-mind when it comes time to reach out to the right artists for the right shows.

Posters and Flyers

Posters used to be a lot more popular and effective back in the days before Facebook, when people actually had to go out into the world to learn about events and happenings in their community. Back then, turning telephone poles and lampposts into public bulletin boards was a great way to promote your event. Back in the '90s, when I was playing in bar bands, Minneapolis passed some sort of "clean city" ordinance that banned flyering and postering on public property. There was an uproar within the local music scene because we could no longer promote gigs by postering the city without risking a fine.

However, posters still have their place, as long as they are posted on public bulletin boards, or on private property with permission. I know that doesn't sound like much fun to those of you with anarchic tendencies, but sometimes you gotta roll with the changes. The local businesses in my current community have been surprisingly supportive when it comes to efforts to publicize creative events in our area. I'm sure the attitudes differ from town to town, and city to city, but I believe that posters can still be utilized—perhaps to a lesser degree than in the past—when it comes time to promote your event.

As for the design of the poster, it's essentially a larger version of your postcard with all the information on one side rather than two. With posters, it's even more important to use one big image with a large headline to capture the attention of your viewers. Unlike postcards, where people are holding them in their hands, posters and flyers must arrest the attention of viewers at a distance.

Resist the temptation to include too much text on your poster/ flyer, and just include the necessary essentials that were mentioned above. That is, tell viewers What is happening, Who is involved, When it's taking place, and Where it's located. With the extra real estate, you may expound a little bit in a way that intrigues and entices the viewer, but don't turn your poster into a novel. Keep it short, keep it punchy and make sure the image/headline combo takes up at least 50% of the space.

Banners

Not every artist will need a banner, but I know several who consistently exhibit work at art fairs, festivals and outdoor events. Each one of them has a large banner that they hang in their booth or at their table to tell their audience exactly who they are and what they do. The competition at fairs and festivals can be pretty fierce, and visitors may not be willing to stop at every booth to view the work. Your banner will attract the visitors' attention from afar, which will draw them in and help them find what they are interested in.

Banner sizes vary and should be created with your specific needs in mind. While I don't care for Vistaprint's free business cards, I have ordered and utilized their banners, which are available in sizes up to 8' wide by 2.5' tall. You can either upload your own artwork (which I only recommend if you have experience producing large-scale graphics), or they have many templates available that you can customize as needed. As far as information goes, you only want the following elements on there: Logo (if you have one), Name or Art Business Name, Tagline or Right Message, and Contact Info.

As for contact info, determine what you want people to do when they see your banner. A phone number or email address may not be the best contact info to include. After all, if the banner draws people to your booth, you can give them a business card. It makes the most sense to include your website address, because visitors who see your banner from across the room are more likely to remember and/or visit a website than remember and/or call a phone number. Plus, you should take every available opportunity to promote your web address.

Other Promotional Items

Earlier in this section, I listed several pieces of business collateral that you may need to utilize depending upon the specific creative field you are in. While I won't go through each one individually, I will say that each piece needs to answer three basic questions:

Who are you? What do you do? How can I reach you?

The elements (logo, name, tagline, contact info, etc.) that answer these questions are secondary to the main function of the individual piece of business collateral, be it a receipt, an invoice, a DVD, a newsletter or a model release. But, in every case, when someone pulls a piece of your collateral out of their pocket, shopping bag, purse or file cabinet, they need to have all the info available to answer the three questions above.

In addition to the essential items we've discussed above, you may want to make a list of both functional and promotional items and tools that you need to run your business. You can find some of the necessary items online by doing a search for items like "invoice template," "artist contract," "model release template," etc. I've also seen packets of business forms at office supply stores like Staples, Office Depot and Office Max that may contain some of the items that pertain to your business.

Software applications like Microsoft Office often have templates within the programs that you can use. When you launch Word or Excel, the Project Gallery window opens, and the left side Category box contains all sorts of templates you can customize.

Or, if you have the design capabilities, you can design all your own collateral. No matter where you get your business collateral, or who designs it, remember: at the end of the day, it ALL needs to be a consistent and cohesive representation of your brand.

Branded Gift Items

Another thing to consider is having some branded promotional items created that feature images of your work, your logo, your website and other pertinent contact info you may want people to have. While this may be unimaginable to the über-serious fine artist, it might be an option for anyone whose work contains a sense of fun, whimsy or humor. There are several websites devoted to print-on-demand products that are both fun and functional, offering a unique way to showcase and share your art (see Resources).

You could offer these items as a prize drawing to reward people for signing up for your mailing list. You can send them as thank-you gifts to people who have helped and supported your art career. You could offer them as raffle prizes at special events and charge one or two dollars for tickets, or you could simply sell them at your openings and events.

It's common in the music industry for a band to make their biggest profits at the merch table, not from the gig or CD sales. For indie filmmakers, having a merch table at film festivals and screenings is a great opportunity to connect with fans who just saw your movie, video or short film and give them a chance to purchase more of your work and take home your contact info via biz cards, postcards, etc. As for artists who show in co-ops, art boutiques and gallery gift shops, having something fun and useful that patrons can take home is yet another way to get your name out there.

Like I said, this option is not for every artist, but if you make the type of art that looks great on a mug or a t-shirt, it's yet another promotional and revenue-generating avenue to explore.

3.8

Press Releases

One of the major benefits of social media is that they empower individuals to build a global network of influential people, with whom they can communicate, engage and share content. While these new media tools provide the individual with amazing reach, utilizing them in tandem with traditional media is still the best way to maximize the effectiveness of your marketing.

The traditional press release is a potent device for bringing your message offline and putting it on the doorstep of your community. Sure, there's a contingent of tech pundits who assert that traditional media is dead, and there are certainly signs of its weakening pulse, but to paraphrase Mark Twain, the reports of its demise are slightly premature.

Here's the kicker: your press release actually has to be good! And by good, I mean well-written, newsworthy and of interest to the community of readers. Getting coverage in traditional media has to be earned, which is why it's referred to as earned media. This is different—and harder—than gaining publicity via social media, where you can publish anything you wish. The following tips and guidelines will increase your chances of getting published with every compelling press release you craft.

Using the Proper Format

It all starts with the format. To a journalist's trained eye, if it don't LOOK like a press release, it ain't a press release. Adhering to the following industry-standard formatting guidelines from PR Syndication will ensure that your press release won't end up in the journalist's circular file (i.e., trash can) at first glance. It still might after she reads it, but at least it won't be due to shoddy and improper structure.

Contact Information – The placement of your press release contact information will depend on your method of distribution. If you are issuing your news to the media using a traditional method, such as mail or fax, place your contact information at the upper left of the page preceding the phrase "FOR IMMEDIATE RELEASE." If you are distributing your press release online, place your contact information at the bottom of the page.

Release Date – If your press release is ready to go live upon distribution, the phrase "FOR IMMEDIATE RELEASE" should appear at the top left of the page, in all caps. If you would prefer journalists to delay publishing your story until a later date, write "HOLD FOR RELEASE UNTIL [Date and Time]" to signal when your news should be announced.

Headline – The headline, or title, of a press release tells readers what the announcement is about. It should be 100 to 150 characters long, and no more than one sentence. Make sure that your headline is carefully worded to grab your audience's attention, and strive to be as creative as possible. Some sources will tell you to use all caps for your headline, but PR Syndication recommends using title case for your headlines.

Capitalize the first letter of all nouns, verbs, adjectives, and adverbs, as well as any prepositions that are four letters or longer. Do not use closing punctuation in headlines, and avoid using exclamation marks anywhere in your press release.

Subhead – A subhead, or subtitle, explains the headline or provides additional relevant details. Subheads are optional; if you are able to convey all pertinent information within the main headline, you do not need to include a subhead.

Dateline – The dateline informs journalists and readers of the press release's origin, and consists of the city, state and date of issue. It should appear in the first line of body copy, preceding the intro sentence and separated by an en-dash with spaces. According to the Associated Press, the dateline should list the city name in all caps, the abbreviated state name, and the full date (including year). Here's an example of how the dateline format should look:

TAMPA, Fla., May 5, 2014 – First sentence of body copy…

Intro and Body Copy – Your press release should begin with a strong introductory paragraph that captures the reader's attention and contains the information most relevant to your message. Always try to include the Five Ws of good journalism—Who, What, When, Where and Why—as applicable. The intro should summarize the key points of your news release, so that even if readers just skim the first paragraph, they'll still understand the highlights of your message. Your intro should engage your audience, and include a hook to entice them to read further. The rest of your body copy can provide more details as well as a quote from a company executive, partner or customer.

It is important to write your announcement from the third-person point of view. Just like a news story, a press release should report on an event, circumstance or occurrence from an objective third-party perspective. Advertising and marketing materials are typically characterized by subjective first-person and second-person copy, so journalists are immediately wary of announcements written from those perspectives. That's why any subjective commentary should be restricted to quotes from a properly attributed source. When writing a news release, always try to think like a journalist.

Boilerplate – The boilerplate is the last paragraph of a press release; it briefly describes the company featured within the announcement. A boilerplate often includes a summary of the company's history, industry, practices and unique value propositions. Add an appropriate subhead such as "About [Company Name]" directly above the boilerplate to visually separate it from the body copy.

Length and Links – (For online press releases only) Ideally, your press release should be 500 to 800 words in length (the total word count includes all text from the headline right down to the close symbol). Aim for 500 words if you have a more simple and straightforward announcement; if you have more details to cover, allow up to 800 words. Search algorithms often factor in link density when scanning online newswires, so your word count should determine the total number of hyperlinks within your press release. The general SEO PR rule of thumb is to include one link per 100 words.

End or Close – A press release should always end with the traditional close symbol "###" (three hashtags) centered at the bottom of the page. This tells journalists and readers that the news release has ended.

Format guidelines Copyright ©2013 PR Syndication. All Rights Reserved.

Press Release in Action

In order to show you how the above formatting looks in an actual example, I've included a press release I wrote for an exhibit called *Pop Culture!* I conceived and co-curated for Liberty Arts Gallery. Not only did this release get published, it also attracted a reporter to the opening reception who wrote a long, detailed follow-up piece that ran the following week.

Study the format guidelines listed above and see if you can spot how and where they come into play in the actual release.

Contact:
Nikolas Allen, Marketing Director
libertyartsgallery@gmail.com
108 Miner Street, Yreka, CA
530-842-0222

FOR IMMEDIATE RELEASE

Liberty Arts Shines a Spotlight on the Iconic and Absurd

YREKA, Ca., March 16, 2011 – What does it take to become a household name, a bona-fide phenomenon, a blip on the radar of American popular culture? Liberty Arts Gallery in Yreka shines a white-hot spotlight on our country's collective fascinations in *Pop Culture! A Celebration of Iconic and Absurd American Obsessions*, opening Friday, April 1.

"I'm a pop culture junkie," admits curator and pop artist Nikolas Allen. "Ever since I was a kid, I've always been fascinated by the cycles of fame and popularity. The apparent randomness of factors that cause people, products and ideas to be exalted on a massive scale is mind-boggling to me."

Co-curator and artist Brenda Woods is a little more skeptical about the cult of popularity.

"Do these things, trends and people really deserve our adulation," she asks, "or are we, as a collective, unconsciously caught up in a wave of hive-mentality euphoria? And will we forget to notice the real world around us if we continually refer to our own superficial and dehumanized icons?"

Despite their different viewpoints on the topic, Allen and Woods have teamed up and set out to create a fun, irreverent spectacle of an exhibit that will evoke emotional connections, nostalgic memories and shared experiences. However, that doesn't mean that all the messages are positive.

"Just because something is popular doesn't mean it's good, constructive, or conducive to our well-being," states Allen. "Some of the pieces speak to our rampant consumerism, our obsession with sex and violence and our total immersion in media and technology."

While the parameters for some of the exhibits at Liberty Arts have been pretty stringent, the *Pop Culture!* parameters were pretty loose: the work had to speak to some element of our popular culture throughout the years—from Little Lulu to Lady Gaga—and/or had to reference, in style or content, the Pop Art movement of the '60s.

Please join Liberty Arts at the Pop Opening Party on Friday, April 1, from 5pm to 8pm, featuring music by DJ Ujjayi, and pop trivia at 6pm.

Liberty Arts is a non-profit, contemporary art gallery providing opportunities for involvement, exposure and action in our community and culture through art. The gallery is open Wednesday through Saturday, from 10am to 5pm, and is located at 108 West Miner Street in Yreka. For more details, visit www.libertyartsyreka.org.

If someone were reading the newspaper at their breakfast table and came across the above article, they would be informed, educated and, hopefully, quite intrigued. These are the objectives you need to meet whenever you write a press release. Think about the audience you are writing for and make every effort to appeal to them while also hitting the Who, What, Where, When, Why points along the way.

How to Make It Newsworthy

Once you've got the formatting down, you need to make sure the content passes the "Why should I care?" test. Editors and journalists have spent their entire careers learning how to be neutral and objective, and everything that comes across their desk needs to hold up to their scrutiny.

Your release actually has to be considered "news" and not come off as a promotional puff piece that doesn't benefit the readers. Some of the following tips and topics have worked well for me and for plenty of other artists when trying to get press.

Community Angle – If your news benefits the community in any way, consider it PR gold. This is especially true when it comes to local newspapers. This could be anything from hosting a local workshop, to offering painting lessons, or producing a public work of art. If you are an active member in your community, the news could even be about something of interest that happened to you, such as receiving an art grant or award or being accepted into a show in a reputable gallery or city outside of your community.

Entertainment Options – People look to community calendars and events pages to get ideas of enjoyable activities to partake in, so a press release about an upcoming show at a local gallery will usually be published if it's written and formatted well. The best part is, once you develop a press-release formula that works, you can simply duplicate that formula and insert the new information rather than having to reinvent the wheel each time.

Human Interest – Generally, people want to read about success stories, so any article using a "local artist makes good" angle can be effective. Same goes for interesting artist profiles, or stories about struggle that end in the artist overcoming the odds and reaching a goal that presented a challenge.

Truly Newsworthy – Once in a while, you may be involved in a project or event that is so different, innovative or new that it truly is considered "news." This happened to me when I was invited to partake in the first Pecha Kucha event in the northern California area.

Pecha Kucha is a creative public event where people present slideshows of anything they are passionate about. All slideshows must conform to a rigid 20 × 20 structure. This means your presentation must contain 20 slides, each shown for 20 seconds, ensuring that everybody's presentation is 6 minutes 40 seconds long. The idea originated with a couple of American architects in Japan, before spreading to other countries overseas and eventually becoming a hot-ticket event in America.

Anybody wanting to host a Pecha Kucha event must get permission from the organization to do so. Therefore, when it came to Redding, California, it was still new and unfamiliar. I wrote a press release with the intention of promoting my own involvement, but slanted the angle as an informative bit of news about this new form of creative expression popping up around the country. My headline was, "Is Pecha Kucha the New Karaoke?" The article was published along with a large color photo of me (i.e., the local artist who was participating in this cool new event in our neighboring city) and met both my promotional and educational objectives.

The above topics and techniques have helped me get dozens of articles published in newspapers, magazines and blogs over the past few years. If I don't have much info on a certain exhibit, I'll keep the press release lean while still hitting the pertinent talking points. On the other hand, if I'm one of the curators or artists in the exhibit or I'm super passionate about the show, or I'm good friends with the artists, I'll dig deeper and expound on certain details and human interest elements, while still keeping to the proven formula.

Building Your PR Contact List

In order to become efficient with your public relations, you need to build a contact list of relevant people working in the media to whom you can quickly and easily submit your press releases. Most galleries will take on the responsibility of promoting an exhibit, but it's best if you take the initiative to do so yourself as well. This will not only guarantee that your events are well-promoted, but it will also impress the gallery, venue or event organizers to see that you are proactive about marketing.

If word gets out that you are responsible for getting great press coverage and bringing your own audience to your events, galleries will actively seek you out, which is a great position to be in.

When building your list, I suggest starting in your own community and growing outward from there. Contact information can usually be found within the publication or on the website of the news outlet you want to reach. Collect the local newspapers, periodicals and magazines in your area and spend some time actually reading them. For the same reason you research galleries before submitting your Artist Packet, you also want to determine if the news outlets you will be targeting are already covering the art scene.

It's also helpful to be somewhat familiar with the style, voice and target audience of each news source so you have a better idea of which ones align best with your audience. This is especially true if you're thinking about paid advertising, but it's even true when you're attempting to get earned media coverage.

Another reason you want to read the periodicals you're targeting is so you can get better at crafting headlines. I mentioned earlier that writing punchy, concise headlines that capture the attention of the reader—and don't merely serve the artist—is an art in itself, and the first reader you need to grab is the editor. If your headline is well-crafted and intriguing enough to draw the editor in, you have a better chance of getting published. They may or may not rewrite your headline, but you've already hooked them, so that's okay. I spend a lot of time on every headline, and even when I've written headlines that felt spot-on, I always encourage the editor to work his own magic to best serve the audience.

When building your PR list, be sure to cover all your bases. There should be several news outlets in your area you can target. Once you're familiar with those, you can target the same types of outlets in different areas when you get shows in other cities and states. Here are a few places to start:

Newspaper – Newspapers vary in content and layout from city to city, but there are usually several potential sections to target, such as Arts & Entertainment, Area News and Community Calendar. Oftentimes, there are different editors for each section, so make sure you get name and contact info for each instead of sending to one general contact. Hitting more targets increases your chances of getting published.

Alternative Papers – In every city there is at least one alt weekly or monthly that has a stronger arts-related focus. Although they are typically owned by large media conglomerates, they do enjoy a little more autonomy and can get more subversive than their mainstream counterparts. The Community Calendar section of these publications is a great target to aim for, because alt weeklies are often the go-to source for people seeking entertainment activities.

Magazines – While you may not want to start out submitting to *Art News*, *Blue Canvas*, *Juxtapoz* and *Hi-Fructose* right out of the gate, you can certainly target them once you've got a few shows under your belt, have put together a great artist packet, or have a killer news release to send. In the meantime, target the magazines popping up in every city that contain more of a localized focus. It seems that producing magazines has become a lot more accessible, so there are more and more titles becoming available all the time. Many of them have a clear niche that targets a certain demographic, and while the arts may not the primary focus of every magazine, most of them do have an Arts section.

The lead times for magazines are longer than for newspapers, so you need to think farther ahead. Speaking of planning ahead, magazines operate on an editorial calendar, and they usually plan out their content up to a year in advance. Knowing what the focus of a certain issue will be is helpful for you when planning your submissions.

Gather the contact info for the appropriate editor and send an exploratory email or phone call. Ask for information about lead times for editorial content (if you plan on submitting a press release article, story or profile piece) and for calendar submissions (if you'll be sending info on events and openings).

Request a copy of their editorial calendar, and while you're at it, ask for a rate card, which provides dimensions and prices of paid advertisements. Remember, magazines are different than newspapers. They exist to sell advertising—especially if they are free, which many of these localized mags are. Editors will be a little more eager to help you out if they think there may be a chance that you will purchase some ad space in the future. And, hey, when the time is right and the money is there, you may want to consider it.

Bloggers – In addition to posting about your events on your own blog, target online outlets such as art, entertainment and culture blogs. This will help you diversify your PR efforts and reach a tech-savvy crowd who may not be reading the local paper or periodicals. As mentioned above, the accessibility of blogging software has allowed anyone with ambition and passion to become a media outlet. Some of these people have managed to build large audiences that would be interested in hearing about your art or your event. Find blogs you enjoy reading and submit your event information and press releases, but don't just send in your PR every month and expect them to publish. Instead, try to spend some time on the blogs leaving comments and adding value and insight to the community. That way, you will become a familiar presence and it may become easier for your items to get published.

If your submissions do get published and people start commenting on them, be sure to reply in a timely manner. You can subscribe to the post so you'll get an email with each comment added, which will tell you when people are engaging with your content. This sounds like a lot of monitoring and maintenance, which is not always possible to do, but it will benefit you to make the effort.

For this reason, it may be best to limit your PR submissions to an amount of media outlets that you can reasonably manage. Focusing on the quality of the outlet in relation to the audience you are trying to reach is better than aiming for sheer quantity.

Local Radio and Cable TV – In many markets, there are community radio and cable television shows that focus on art and entertainment events that are happening in the area. They are often run from college campuses or community television stations and, in addition to sharing calendar-type event info, some of the programs even interview guests. Scout out the programs that focus on art, culture or entertainment, and find out who the producers, hosts or deejays are and submit your information directly to them.

Be sure to make your objectives clear when submitting. Whether you're sending opening reception information to the radio for a community calendar–type announcement, or requesting an interview on a local cable TV art program, state your request clearly in your submission and let them know what their next steps should be if they are interested. Always include your complete contact information—as was stated in the PR formatting guidelines—and encourage your recipient to contact you if they have any questions or want to follow up for more info.

Online PR Submissions – In addition to the targets mentioned above, there are also several online targets you may wish to consider when submitting PR. The first would be the online versions of the printed periodicals you are targeting. For example, you can submit a press release to the editor of your local newspaper and he may or may not decide to run it. But the online version of the same paper has a community calendar section that allows people to post their own events.

Therefore, you should also post a condensed version of the event to the newspaper's website, in order to make sure your bases are covered. Same goes for the alt weeklies, and even the magazines. When compiling your list of PR targets, be sure to investigate their online and offline properties, so you can double up your efforts and increase your chance of getting published and reaching your audience.

If any of the arts councils, co-ops or organizations in your area post events on their website, or send out notices in their email, be sure to submit to them as well. Arts councils work extra hard to develop, sustain and promote the arts, so it's beneficial to connect with them, especially in the early stages of your career. If you're living in a smaller market, connecting with an arts council will help you to feel solidarity with like-minded people so you don't feel like you're going it alone.

In some cases you may have to be a member in order to reap the promotional rewards (we discussed this in an earlier section), but not all cases. Keep in mind that by becoming a member, you are supporting an organization that exists to help facilitate creativity and enrich culture. To me, that's always worth supporting.

There are many websites devoted to promoting events in different regions, and some of them may be worth investigating. However, it's easy to get overwhelmed with all the choices, so I would recommend building your list of online PR targets slowly over time. Start by submitting to the sites you are certain will reach your target audience, and keep an eye out for other outlets along the way.

One thing I would adamantly suggest is to avoid Craigslist at all costs. Throughout the early- and mid-aughts, it was actually a great platform for finding talent and connecting with people, but has since devolved into a bottom-of-the-barrel quagmire of spammers, scammers and vampires looking to leech off anyone stupid enough to still be found there. This opinion—both the good and the bad—is based on personal experience, and while your experience may vary, I will never use it or even recommend it to anyone ever again. If you choose to use it, proceed at your own risk.

Don't Forget to Show Your Appreciation

One way to build relationships with journalists, editors and bloggers is to show your appreciation when they do publish your submissions. Media outlets are responsible for producing tons of content. If you submit the occasional story that will make their jobs easier, they will appreciate it. However, that doesn't mean they are obligated to give you press. You still need to earn it. That can be done either by submitting a well-written, relevant article they can use, or by doing remarkable things in the art world that they cannot ignore.

Then, when they do publish articles, stories or event listings that mention you and your art, show them your appreciation. This completes the cycle of communication, leaves them with a positive impression, and will help them remember you next time your name pops up in their inbox.

Sending a simple email thanking your contact for the mention, write-up or article will suffice, but they get so many emails, it's nice to send them something they will remember. After getting an important article published, I like sending postcards to my contact person. This is another reason to get physical addresses in addition to email addresses when you are building your list of PR contacts.

Earlier we talked about creating postcards that feature your own work on the front, and this is the perfect time to put them to use. Sending a card is an easy way to stand out, because the majority of people they deal with will not contact them afterwards to say "thank you." But you will, because you're an art-marketing superstar!

> When I was curating the "Pop Culture" exhibit at Liberty Arts Gallery, the local paper printed my press release a couple of weeks prior to the show. Then, a few days before the opening, my co-curator and I visited the newspaper offices with pastries, a pound of freshly ground coffee beans, and a stack of "Pop Culture" postcards promoting the show. We also taped postcards to the coffee bag and pastry box so everyone enjoying the treats would know where they came from. The paper sent a reporter to the opening, who shot great photographs, interviewed the curators and several artists, and printed a glowing follow-up review the following week.

When building your list of PR contacts, start with a focus on local media outlets because it makes the most sense to interest readers in your own area to come to your shows. As you start expanding your circle of influence, build your contact list along with your growth. If you've written a great press release or article about you and your work—whether it's an introductory profile or it details an innovative approach or technique that would be of interest to the art world in general—then by all means target some of the bigger media outlets that cover the artists you enjoy reading about. Submitting your PR to the press is similar to submitting your art to galleries, in that the more media outlets, venues and publications you contact, the better your chances of being published. As your career trajectory grows, you may get representation, the press may start seeking you for profiles and interviews, and the galleries you work with may bear most of the responsibility of advertising and promoting you and your show.

But until you reach that point, it's up to you to be proactive with your publicity, your advertising, your networking and your marketing. It's a big responsibility for artists who would rather hang out in their studio, getting lost in their own creative process for months on end, but it will mean the difference between actively going out and capturing the attention of the art world, or passively waiting for the art world to notice you.

Personally, when it comes to my own career, I'll take active over passive any day. How about you?

 **Download the free DTSA Workbook to create your own custom art-marketing strategy:**

www.DeathToTheStarvingArtist.com/workbook

EPILOGUE
PREPARING FOR THE MARATHON

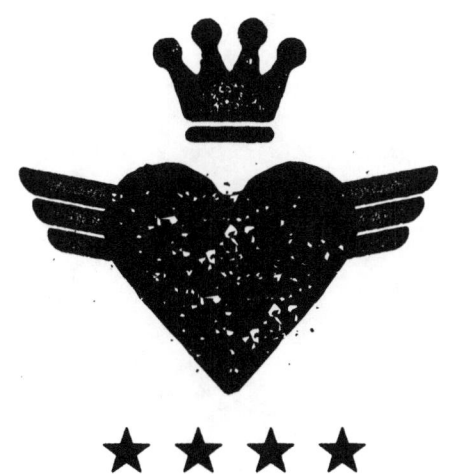

★ ★ ★ ★

E.1

Are You Ready to Go the Distance?

I've met people who call themselves artists, yet have painted less than a dozen canvases. That's okay, because you have to start somewhere. However, while these people may very well have artistic talent, and technical or creative skill, there's a difference between dabbling in the studio, and dedicating a portion of one's life to the pursuit of creative expression. Just like there's a difference between throwing your sneakers on for a sprint down the block, and training several months for a multi-mile marathon.

Obviously, pursuing a career in art is a long-term commitment. It's a marathon, and so is marketing. Some people get frustrated after creating a few pieces of art, and they give up hope of being successful. I see many people—artists and business owners alike—who adopt a few marketing techniques, only to bail out when they don't see immediate progress. In either case, you have to be in it to win it, just like those dedicated runners who enter the marathon.

After reading about the abundance of tools, tactics and strategies listed throughout this book, you may feel a bit overwhelmed. It will make you feel better to realize that you don't need to implement them all. While it will be up to you to decide which of the aforementioned tactics, strategies and platforms you use, remember that your objectives will play a large part in helping determine your choices. We started this book discussing objectives for a reason! Take the time to clearly define your objectives before you do anything. Then pick and choose a few of the tools and techniques that are appropriate to help you reach the people you want to reach, with the message you want to send, and start there. Keep track of what is working and what is not, and if something isn't working after several months or a year, then don't be afraid to drop it.

I took a marketing workshop several years ago, and two bits of advice I got from the instructor have stuck with me ever since. The first bit was, "Use what's working and drop the rest!" A very simple conceit, yet powerful and liberating at the same time. Applying this advice empowers you to clean out your marketing toolbox occasionally, and free up room for new tools and tactics. However, it's best if you replace the things you drop with something else you haven't tried yet.

Also, it's important to allow ample time to see results before declaring something ineffective. If you change things too quickly, whether it's your target audience, your tools or your message, you won't have enough information to know if the ones you gave up on were truly right for you or not.

The second bit of advice that stuck was, "Don't be afraid to let your business become something you didn't expect." At the time I took this workshop, I was still trying to build a business selling screenprinted apparel for the female youth market that featured my designs. I had sold a decent amount but wanted to turn it into a sustainable long-term business. When that didn't happen, I took my instructor's advice and started a marketing consulting business that aimed to help artists and business owners improve their marketing and grow their business.

While I was taking this workshop, I never would have guessed that I would head in that direction, but I took that advice to heart when the time was right. These days, I'm a fully self-employed marketing consultant, AND still exhibiting and selling my fine art products through select gallery showings and events.

As for applying this advice to your career, there are certain styles or disciplines of art that catch on for whatever reason. For example, let's say you are a painter who creates large, dramatic abstracts, but you also enjoy making birdhouses out of pinecones and driftwood. Then, on a whim, you enter your birdhouses into an art fair and they are a hit with the public. Don't discount the obvious; embrace the opportunity. Go with what works, and don't be afraid to head in a direction that you did not expect. Don't let feelings of fear, guilt or doubt block you from creating work that people want to buy.

There's nothing more pathetic than people who strive so hard to "keep it real" that they fight, kick and scream to avoid any type of recognition or success. Kurt Cobain was a great example of this. Privately, he had great aspirations to be in the biggest band on the planet. Publicly, he railed against his band's success, the commercialization of his music and the corporate machination that his band had to endure. Then, when his band actually became the biggest on the planet, he couldn't handle the pressure that came along with it.

You cannot simultaneously strive for and reject something. If you want to make art purely as creative expression, fine, go for it. But if that's the case, you need to put ALL thoughts of commerce, business, success, fame or recognition out of your mind and simply make your art. And if that's the case, you'd better plan on making your money elsewhere, because you cannot have it both ways. You cannot attempt to achieve success while maintaining the pose that you actually disdain it.

Conversely, if you want to make art that is truly an expression of your creative soul, AND embrace the idea that it's perfectly okay to make an effort to sell it, for people to buy it, and for you to treat your art as a business endeavor, then you must unabashedly maintain that attitude as you move towards your goals. Sure, you will come across people (mostly other artists) who resent your pro-commerce attitude, cast aspersions on the purity of your work, and question and criticize your motives, but you cannot let those outside opinions affect or change your stance one iota.

Artists carry around their own personal dogma regarding the importance of art, the purity of expression and the evils of soiling the integrity of creativity through commercial pursuits. This is part of the Starving Artist paradigm that I believe needs to be eradicated. There is nothing noble about "suffering for your art" or slogging miserably through life while you "pay your dues." This is why many great artists have wound up broke and bitter, pissed off at a world they see as "unjust and unfair." Perhaps the problem did not lie in the world, but rather in them.

Can you sell tons of work and still maintain your own creative and personal integrity? Absolutely! Success and integrity are not mutually exclusive. It's more about your personal character. If you create art as a true expression of your being, and allow your own values to dictate your business decisions, you will be able to maintain your integrity regardless of how much money you make from your art. This should be your ultimate goal.

The Most Important Marketing Element

The most important element of your marketing is YOU. That means it is imperative for you to be present at the important networking opportunities in your field. That could be art openings, rock shows, film screenings, dance performances, conferences, symposiums, workshops, etc.

However, you should still be selective. If you're out hobnobbing every weekend, it may be detracting from precious time that you could be using to create your own work. In my mind, the act of creating your own work almost always takes precedence.

When you are out networking, be prepared. Have your business cards, postcards or pertinent promo materials handy. Carry a pen, a small pad, a smartphone, camera, digital recorder— whatever tools you prefer to use for capturing contacts, ideas, inspiration and relevant info.

If I may get a little esoteric here, I've experienced enough of life to realize that we are not completely in control of our own destiny. No matter how hard you work, push, kick, scream, dream or scheme something into existence, there's an unseen variable involved—some call it 'fate'—that leads you in the exact direction you are supposed to go in your life. Sometimes it leads gently, other times it kicks your ass six ways to Sunday. I believe that there are certain lessons we are born into this life to learn, and each of our lives provides us with the exact circumstances and opportunities required to learn those lessons. The people who are savvy enough to see these lessons, to learn from them and to alter their behaviors accordingly, move on, advance, progress. The people who are too dense to "get it" continue making the same poor choices and stupid mistakes. They do not pass GO. They do not collect $200.

There have been many times I was absolutely, positively certain I was on the right path, perfectly poised, positioned and prepared for that "big, game-changing break" or "next-level success," only to be met with a chorus of crickets, chirping away as my confidence dripped to the floor like high-viscosity latex paint off fresh canvas, smearing the vision of my dreams along the way.

I've spent many hours pondering how someone like Justin Bieber can blow up, seemingly overnight, at the tender age of 15 on the strength of a few home videos discovered on YouTube, while many, many other far more talented and experienced artists of all media languish in obscurity their whole lives. It's not solely about talent. There are millions of talented people in the world. It's not even about "right place, right time," which I mentioned earlier in this book. There is a famous quote attributed to Zig Ziglar that says, "Success is when preparation meets opportunity." While that is certainly true, I believe this quote should contain the addendum, "...with a little magic pixie dust sprinkled on top."

Don't get me wrong, I'm not suggesting you wait around waiting for "fate" to sweep you into the stratosphere of success. Nor am I suggesting you shake your fist at the heavens, curse the gods for not sprinkling magic pixie dust on your life, and slump into a corner as the featured guest of your own pity party. I'm suggesting that you pursue your dreams with all your passion, all your efforts, all your talents and skills.

Understand that you yourself have been created as a work of art—by a great, unseen artist—to fulfill a Purpose in life that only you can fulfill. That may have everything to do with your art, and it may have nothing to do with your art, but as an artist who has been blessed with the gift of creativity, you should continue to exercise your gift, regardless of the outcome. If the flame of artistic passion burns within you, give it an outlet—don't let it consume you in a fiery blaze of inertia. As a well-known phrase states, "don't die with a song still in your heart." Or, as I wrote in one of my own songs, "don't let the ship sink with all of your treasure on board."

Learn the principles outlined in this book, allow yourself to be inspired, continue to apply the knowledge and lessons you pick up throughout your life. Embrace change. Embrace opportunity. Create. Love. Live. Be generous in sharing your gifts with the world. Forget the critics. Forget the haters and nay-sayers. Exist with integrity and enjoy each moment of this wild ride called Life. Release your self-limitations. Kill your inner critic. Open your heart, your mind, and the secret treasure chest that holds all your magical concepts, ideas and creations, and spill them out on the canvas, on the stage, on the screen.

Let go of the belief that there is nobility in struggle. Obliterate the idea that selling art equals selling out. Temper your own expectations of what should be by fully accepting what is. Rise up out of the primordial muck of self-doubt, self-hatred, self-criticism and take a long, hard look at yourself in the mirror.

You should see a magnificent, unique, singular, powerful human being starting back at you. An Artist. A Creator. A Harvester of Ideas. And if you don't? If you still see a Starving Artist gaping at you with its hollow eyes, pitiful smirk and constricted heart… kill it once and for all.

RESOURCES

R.1

Art Marketing Resources

The websites listed below correspond to some of the categories I mentioned throughout the book. This list will give you plenty of places to start in the categories you are researching. I have used some of these services but not all, so it will be up to you to visit the sites to see which ones resonate with you. There are many options available but you only need to find a handful of reliable sources that you can continue to use as needed.

You will notice I don't put "www" in front of each web address. As I mention in the book, browsers are smart enough to not need them. Simply punching in the URLs as listed below will take you to the sites.

Artist Portfolio Sites
Artsy Shark... artsyshark.com
Behance..behance.net
Deviant Art.. deviantart.com
Saatchi Online .... saatchionline.com
Squarespace .... squarespace.com

Artist Resource Sites
Art Biz Blog... artbizblog.com
Artists Who Thrive................................. artistswhothrive.com
Death To The Starving Artist ... deathtothestarvingartist.com
Empty Easel..emptyeasel.com
Fine Art Views ....fineartviews.com
Skinny Artist .... skinnyartist.com

Domain Names

Enom .... enom.com
Go Daddy .... godaddy.com
Net Firms.. netfirms.com

Email Marketing Platforms

Aweber .... aweber.com
Constant Contact................................... constantcontact.com
Exact Target.. exacttarget.com
iContact .... icontact.com
Mail Chimp .... mailchimp.com

Fonts

1001 Fonts 1001fonts.com
DaFont .... dafont.com
Font Squirrel ....fontsquirrel.com

Hosting Companies

Go Daddy .... godaddy.com
Host Gator .... hostgator.com
Host Monster .... hostmonster.com
Host Papa.. hostpapa.com

Logo Design

99 Designs 99designs.com
Fuel My Brand ....fuelmybrand.com
Logo Design Team.................................. logodesignteam.com
Logo Snap ....logosnap.com

Mailing List Opt-In Forms

Pippity.. pippity.com
Pop-Up Domination .... popupdomination.com

Mobile Payment Platforms

Flint .... flint.com
PayPal...paypal.com
Square.. squareup.com

Naming

Business Name Generator .... businessnamegenerator.com
Name Thingy... namethingy.com
Naming ....naming.net
Panabee...panabee.com
Thesaurus.. thesaurus.com

Online Arts Councils

I'm including California because it's a great West Coast resource.
A quick Google search will give you the URL of Arts Councils in
your preferred target area.

California Arts Council.. cac.ca.gov

Online Galleries

Art 3000 .... art-3000.com
Art Dot Com .... art.com
Artspace..artspace.com
Artspan .... artspan.com
Etsy...etsy.com
Rise Art .... riseart.com
UGallery .... ugallery.com

Online Print Shops

1-800Postcards.. 1800postcards.com
Got Print...gotprint.com
Moo .... moo.com
PsPrint...psprint.com
Vista Print... vistaprint.com

Press Release Services

24-7 Press Release.................................24-7pressrelease.com
PR Buzz...prbuzz.com
PR Log...prlog.com
PR Web .... prweb.com

Promotional Items

Branded Gear .... brandedgear.com
Branders...branders.com
Café Press... cafepress.com
Halo Branded Solutions..halo.com
Zazzle ....zazzle.com

QR Code Generators

Go QR .... goqr.me
Kaywa... qrcode.kaywa.com
The QR Code Generator................the-qrcode-generator.com

QR Code Readers

Available for download from your preferred smartphone app store

Taxes

How to get a reseller's license.....................................
salehoo.com/blog/how-to-get-a-reseller-license-sales-tax-id

WordPress

Self-hosted sites and blogs................................... wordpress.org
WordPress-hosted sites and blogs .... wordpress.com
WordPress Plug-Ins............................ wordpress.org/plug-ins

WordPress Themes

Elegant Themes.. elegantthemes.com
Ink Themes..inkthemes.com
Organic Themes....................................... organicthemes.com
Studio Press .... studiopress.com
Theme Forest.. themeforest.com
Themes Kingdom ....themeskingdom.com
Wordpress... wordpress.org/themes

 **Download the free DTSA Workbook to create your own custom art-marketing strategy:**

www.DeathToTheStarvingArtist.com/workbook

About The Author

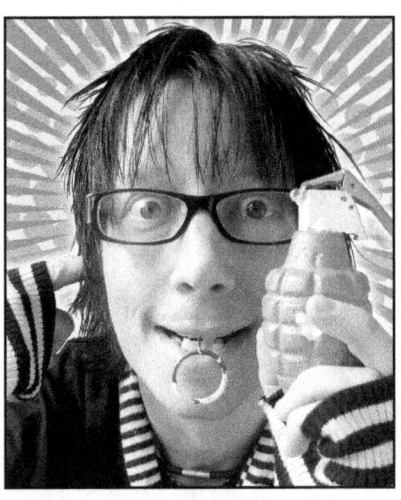

Nikolas Allen

Nikolas Allen is a contemporary pop artist who creates bold, fun, irreverent works of art in various media. Over the years, he has expressed his creativity through writing, drawing, painting, photography, graphic design, filmmaking, poetry and music. Some of these ventures have been commercial pursuits and others have been for the pure thrill of creative expression. Unlike many "purists," he believes art and commerce make awesome bedfellows.

He has also enjoyed a twenty-year career in advertising that has instilled a deep passion for branding, marketing and the entrepreneurial spirit. In 2010, Nikolas combined his passion for these topics and launched BAM! Small Biz Consulting to help small business owners reach a wider audience through effective online and offline marketing strategies. Since many of his clients were artists, he started teaching art-marketing workshops, from which emerged the outline that became this book.

Nikolas has lived in Greece, Africa, Minnesota, Louisiana, Texas, and New Mexico. He currently resides at the foot of a magical, mystical volcano in the far reaches of northern California where the air is clean, the water is pure and the art is...rustic.

To contact the artist, visit: nikolasallen.com
To contact the author, visit: deathtothestarvingartist.com

www.ingramcontent.com/pod-product-compliance
Lightning Source LLC
Chambersburg PA
CBHW051453170526
45166CB00001B/221